SECRET OF MY SUCCESS

JAMIE X OLIVER

Viva Books

New Delhi | Mumbai | Chennai | Kolkata | Bangalore | Hyderabad | Kochi | Guwahati

First Indian Edition 2010

VIVA BOOKS PRIVATE LIMITED

- 4737/23 Ansari Road, Daryaganj, New Delhi 110 002
  E-mail: vivadelhi@vivagroupindia.net, Tel. 42242200
- 76, Service Industries, Shirvane, Sector 1, Nerul, Navi Mumbai 400 706
  E-mail: vivamumbai@vivagroupindia.net, Tel. 27721273, 27721274
- Jamals Fazal Chambers, 26 Greams Road, Chennai 600 006
  E-mail: vivachennai@vivagroupindia.net, Tel. 28290304, 28294241
- B-103, Jindal Towers, 21/1A/3 Darga Road, Kolkata 700 017
  E-mail: vivakolkata@vivagroupindia.net, Tel. 22836381, 22816713
- 7, Sovereign Park Apartments, 56-58, K. R. Road, Basavanagudi, Bangalore 560 004
  E-mail: vivabangalore@vivagroupindia.net, Tel. 26607409, 26607410
- 101-102 Mughal Marc Apartments, 3-4-637 to 641, Narayanguda, Hyderabad 500 029
  E-mail: vivahyderabad@vivagroupindia.net, Tel. 27564481, 27564482
- Beevi Towers, First Floor, SRM Road, Kaloor, Kochi 682 018, Kerala
  E-mail: vivakochi@vivagroupindia.net, Tel: 0484-2403055, 2403056
- 232, GNB Road, Beside UCO Bank, Silpukhuri, Guwahati 781 003
  E-mail: vivaguwahati@vivagroupindia.net, Tel: 0361-2666386

www.vivagroupindia.com

Published by arrangement with

Crimson Publishing,
a division of Crimson Business Ltd
Westminster House, Kew Road
Richmond, Surrey TW9 2ND

ISBN : 978-81-309-1522-7

Published by Vinod Vasishtha for Viva Books Private Limited, 4737/23, Ansari Road, Daryaganj, New Delhi - 110 002.

Printed and bound by Raj Press, R-3, Inderpuri, New Delhi - 110 012.

CONTENTS

NETWORKING

LEADERSHIP

Introduction

Richard Branson started his business life sitting in a crypt, mailing records to teenagers. Then along came a postal strike threatening the fledgling company. The entrepreneur behind US coffee chain giant Starbucks, Howard Schultz, sent out 223 funding proposals without securing any backing. *Dragons' Den* entrepreneur Theo Paphitis lost his entire business as a result of the stock market crash of the late eighties, early nineties.

Branson's response to the crisis was to open a record shop on London's Oxford Street under the name Virgin records. Howard Schultz sent out proposal number 224 and at last received the funding he was looking for. Theo Paphitis took stock, gathered his thoughts, and embarked on the business journey that today makes him one of the UK's best-known entrepreneurs.

Adversity made all three stronger through a mix of persistence, determination and having faith in their vision. In these trying economic times, these characteristics are vital attributes of success. So is there a secret of success? Well, the secret is, there are no secrets. Most successful entrepreneurs will tell you it boils down to hard work and a dollop of luck.

Enthusiasm for a new business will get you a long way, but the successful entrepreneurs all have good people around them. They understand their own weaknesses and get the best people they can possibly afford in the positions that count. Sales, cashflow, marketing – all these things are critical to the success of a business, but no one is expert at everything. Successful entrepreneurs understand that.

Most business founders I've interviewed would agree that they are unemployable. That's not to say they're not good people, it's just they have their own views on how things should be done. One reason most start out in business is because they think a product or service can be made better, cheaper or more effective.

Entrepreneurship is something that all school children should be taught, because it can be learned. There are rules, reasons and above all, there is a whole lot of potential out there that could be harnessed by the entrepreneurs of tomorrow to make this world a better place.

While current economic conditions remain difficult, one thing that sets successful entrepreneurs apart is their ability to take advantage of even the most trying financial circumstances. Most of those interviewed for this book have seen the good times and bad – and most would agree that it is in the hard times that they learned those vital business lessons about concentrating on bottom line results. As the sage of Omaha, Warren Buffett puts it: 'It's only when the tide goes out that you learn who's been swimming naked'. Ultimately, it's the critical entrepreneurial traits – determination and perseverance – that are even more important in hard times.

Hopefully this book will help impart some expertise and know-how from entrepreneurs who have made it that you can apply to your business.

Jamie Oliver's Secrets of Success columns appeared in The Daily Telegraph's business section between 2007 and 2009. All financial information in the articles was correct at the time of publication.

ATTITUDE

"I would rather hire a man with enthusiasm, than a man who knows everything"

John D. Rockefeller, industrialist and philanthropist

Howard Schultz

'I need to be authentic, honest and open'

When asked for the secrets of his success, Starbucks CEO Howard Schultz says luck played a big part. In 1982, his plan was to open a chain of 100 coffee houses across the US, but Schultz says:

'I had real trouble raising private equity money. It was very difficult. In fact I had to downsize the number of outlets I hoped to open from 100 to 75, but I couldn't afford to have the prospectuses reprinted, so I crossed the 100 out by hand and wrote in 75. It simply hadn't been done and here was I trying to convince people to invest in this plan for a national chain of coffee houses and one that was planning to offer all staff health insurance and a stake in the business. I was turned down by 224 people – I've got a dossier to prove it.'

So while luck played a part, persistence and determination were key. But, in explaining how to persevere from knock-back number 221, Schultz says:

'We believed. We were passionate and we almost willed it to happen. There was nothing like what we were looking to offer, which was a third place – a place between your home and your work. We had no money for advertising so needed people to spread the word through word-of-mouth. Our people and our customers became our ambassadors.'

It's been an incredible journey for the 55-year-old, New York-born Schultz. He grew up in a housing project in Brooklyn, New York, and attended Northern Michigan University on a football scholarship. Schultz played quarterback, which was good, he says, but painful. He graduated from college with a communications degree and then joined Zerox, before becoming a general manager at a business that supplied non-electric coffee machines to Starbucks. In 1982, he joined Starbucks Coffee Company in Seattle as the director of marketing but had ideas and plans for the business that the founders didn't share. So he left and set up a rival coffee house chain, called Il Giornale. In 1987, the original owners of Starbucks sold out to Schultz and he rebranded Il Giornale to Starbucks.

Today, the ubiquitous coffee shop chain operates 700 stores in the UK, more than 16,000 globally and had fourth quarter revenues in 2008 of around $2.5bn. While coffee is not immune from the harsh economic conditions – profit for the last three months of the year fell to $5.4m, compared with $158.5m for the same period the year before – Schultz is confident his business and the brand can ride out the recession. He says:

'It will be a difficult period ahead. But it's not the first time we've faced difficulties. 1986 was a difficult year. My wife was pregnant with our first child and I wasn't taking a salary. It was tough to cover the payroll and hard to pay vendors. In fact, one day my wife's father came to see me in Seattle. We sat on a park bench and he said to me, "You've got to give up this hobby and get a proper job".'

Schultz wisely ignored his father-in-law.

Schultz says that 'hiring ahead of the curve' has helped his business grow, in that he hires people with skills he doesn't possess. 'I also think giving people a stake in the business has helped us get where we are today.'

He says he is more mindful than ever of his responsibilities to a wide range of constituents, especially shareholders and, that day-to-day, his role is all about communicating.

'For me, as CEO, it's about being as visible as possible to employees and all parts of the business. I need to communicate more than ever. I travel a great deal. I need to be present and available to people. I need to be authentic, honest and open. People need to be told the truth about what we're doing. This is no time for spin.'

He dismisses accusations of anti-competitive behaviour. He says:

'I'm happy with the way we have expanded. It's fun. We've become part of culture around the world and it's all very positive. We're in 48 countries and relevant in places I could never have imagined, such as China, the Middle East, Japan and Singapore. We've just opened our first store in Bulgaria. What we've created is not American. It has a universal appeal. People drink coffee around the world and it appeals to people.'

Schultz is also direct when it comes to accusations of being in some way guilty of exploiting coffee farmers.

'We have created an industry, jobs, a whole supply chain that didn't exist,' he says. 'Thousands of people have benefited from this company and we do more for coffee growers than the rest of the industry put together. We offer healthcare to workers and ownership to staff both in the US and here. We use our size as a positive thing.'

He says that when things are tough for him, he talks to lifelong friends, and people who are in a similar position to him. 'I talk to my family, of course, but ultimately, it's down to me. I have to listen to my own voice.'

What advice does he have for other business owners?

'You need to be a visible and present leader. We had a meeting in the US recently, attended by 1,000 Starbucks store owners. I also travel a lot, I do media, we do emails to staff, webcasts. I try to be open and honest with people and I try to ensure that all employees share the vision of this company. That means they each have a role and each have responsibilities. Every single person is accountable.'

William Chase

'Have a passion for your business'

William Chase, the founder of Tyrrells Potato Chips, offers a rapid-fire, bullet point summary of his business life story:

'I was born on a farm in Herefordshire, UK, dropped out of university aged 20, then borrowed £200,000 from the bank to buy a potato farm. By 1992, my bank was charging me 27% interest and I went bankrupt. In 1993 I started again with nothing – minus nothing really, because to be a bankrupt in rural Herefordshire was like being a leper. In the 1990s I was trading potatoes and dealing them to the big supermarkets, but I saw the end coming for local producers and started looking into making other potato-related products.'

It was at this point Chase moved into the manufacture of potato chips. Tyrrells also make vegetable chips, apple chips and a range of dips. Today the business employs 120 people, has a turnover of £15m and is continually expanding into new markets, new territories and new products. For his next venture Chase plans to produce potato vodka.

'Someone said to me once, it's not turnover that's important, it's leftover. I think that's right. You see these enormous companies turning over millions or billions and they are making a tiny percentage on all that work. But we make 25%.' Chase says that Tyrrells account for about 2% of the billion pound crisp or chip market, while the vodka market is worth £10bn – and Tyrrells wants a slug of that.

Chase continues enthusiastically:

'We're a small business and we're like a speedboat. We can change direction easily and react to events. I'd say the hardest thing is making the first £100,000. Stelios has done incredibly well but he never had to do that. Whereas someone like British vacuum cleaner inventor James Dyson, now there is a man who I admire.'

Chase says communication with people is important, but it is more important to know how to turn 50p into £1, something he reckons he didn't really understand until he was in his late-thirties.

'A lot of people in this country are in the wrong job. I used to work in potatoes and could have stayed doing that but I spotted an opportunity and went for it. I'm involved in all aspects of the business, such as the PR and marketing, the design of the packaging. I did the packaging because no agency really understood the business, and what we were trying to do, better than me. I do find it hard to step back. I admit that, but I've just got an MD in to run the business and it has freed me up to do other things.'

What is obvious about Chase is his passion and excitement for the award-winning business. He says, 'I look forward to work and really love it. I think a lot of people who work here love it too, and that's how it should be if you're spending most of your waking hours doing something.'

When it comes to hiring or working with like-minded souls, Chase says he looks for charisma. 'People come and see me sometimes, salespeople for example, and they pull out their laptop and go through a PowerPoint presentation. You know what? It makes me shudder. I can't stand it.'

Trevor Sorbie

'It's about not diluting myself'

'I'd never get out of bed for a £1 note. I'd only get out of bed to do a haircut,' says Trevor Sorbie, one of the best-known hairdressers in the world. Sorbie started life in a tenement block in Paisley, Scotland. He had mince and potatoes for Christmas dinner and every Friday night he would share the tin bath with his brother. He says, 'I've never forgotten that. It's made me grounded throughout my life and very appreciative of everything I've got.'

Leaving school at the age of 15, Sorbie worked in his father's barbers but the two ended up 'getting on each other's nerves'. His dad then set him up in his own barbers when Sorbie was 20 but, by his own admission, he was 'sick of hairdressing'. Instead of giving up, he decided to concentrate on ladies hair and enrolled in a course at the Richard Henry School of Hairdressing. Spotted as talent by the principal, Sorbie went on to work for some of the biggest names in hairdressing, no more so than Vidal Sassoon in central London.

Talking about his time at Sassoon, Sorbie says:

'Some of the best hairdressers in the world worked at Sassoon. When I worked there, I didn't sit in the staff room during my breaks. I stood on the floor and watched them work. But, you know, there are things in life that you will never be able do; bungee jumping, for example. I could never do that. But as I stood and watched these great hairdressers, I thought that if I worked hard there was no reason why I couldn't get to their level.'

Sorbie's studies were rewarded. When Sassoon was asked to do a show in Paris, the creative directors, of which Sorbie was one, were asked to come up with new hairstyles. Sorbie created 'The Wedge', a hairstyle later sported by the likes of David Bowie and in that moment, 'a jaw-dropping moment', Sorbie knew he had arrived. He now runs two salons, in London and Brighton, puts his name to a series of hair product ranges, has been British hairdresser of the year on countless occasions, was awarded an MBE in 2004 and became an Ambassador for Hairdressers of the World Against Aids in 2006.

'I could open five, 10, 20 more salons,' Sorbie says, 'but for me it's about not diluting myself. I could make more money but I'd lose the quality and I'm not prepared to do that.'

He admits he can't read a profit and loss sheet but believes in getting people working with him who can do what he can't. 'I have a business partner who's been with me for longer than both of my marriages,' Sorbie says, 'and we're not even great friends. It's just that he goes to bed thinking about making money and I go to bed thinking about creating great hair styles.'

Loyalty is important to Sorbie, who says:

'I've got a hairdresser who works with me that has been here for 13 years. That's rare. Why do people stay here? It's the quality of the work we do, the customer service we offer. People who come here for a job know that once they work for me they will be able to get a job in any salon in the world.'

'If Nicky Clarke fell on hard times and came to me wanting a job, even though he's a friend, he wouldn't just walk into one. He'd have to be interviewed to see that we got on; he'd then have to do five different hairstyles, then be trained by me for two months, then do a final exam of nine different hairstyles. If he went to any other salon outside London with his £10,000 worth of customers he'd get a job straight away. But not here.'

David Giampaolo

'Great entrepreneurs wake up in the morning and say "it's not working, let's change it"'

'Entrepreneurs need tenacity, patience and realism,' says David Giampaolo. And one of these qualities was in evidence when he came to the UK from the US to set up the first in a planned chain of fitness clubs in 1998. 'We wrote to Buckingham Palace and asked if Princess Diana would come and open the first gym,' he says. 'To our amazement, she did.' The resulting publicity helped the business become a massive success for Giampaolo – he sold it six years later for £840m.

Giampaolo got into the fitness business because he was a fitness enthusiast. One day, while at his gym in the US, he wondered whether the place couldn't be done a whole lot better than it was and, speaking his thoughts out loud, turned to fellow gym-goers. The two, who were doctors, said to Giampaolo if he had the energy to do it, they had the money to invest. It was the start of a lifetime love affair with private equity.

Today, American Giampaolo is chief executive of Pi Capital, a private equity firm he led the acquisition of in 2002. It invests in profitable companies requiring between £2m and £5m of equity. Pi Capital is also a network of successful and influential business people, who between them sit on more than 600 company boards. Members are based in Europe, the US and Asia and the estimated investment firepower of Pi members is put at 'up to £10bn'.

It all puts Giampaolo in a rare position. Not only has he been a successful entrepreneur in his own right, he now knows some of the brightest entrepreneurial and business talent there is and is constantly on the lookout for up-and-coming businesses in which he and his associates can invest. He knows all about risk, failure, hard work and luck, admits that he could easily fill 24 hours a day working if it was physically possible and that he struggles sometimes to switch off (his tip: go to the cinema).

Seeing up to 100 business plans a month on the hunt for investment also means that he understands what makes a successful company. 'Management. They need to be hungry, passionate, smart, humble and want to offer a world-class product or service that is needed or better than what is on offer.' He looks at managers' reputations, their goals, even their marital status. 'If someone isn't an optimist in life they will find it hard to succeed in business,' he says. 'But of course there are degrees of optimism.'

Being a successful entrepreneur, according to Giampaolo, requires the skills of a world-class plate spinner. He says:

'It's good to have lots of plates spinning. It creates optimality. It means you have options. A lot of the most outstanding entrepreneurs will appear as though they are putting the farm on a deal but you can bet they have a Plan B and C if things go wrong. Entrepreneurs are risk-takers, yes, but it is very calculated.'

Giampaolo gets an interesting insight into entrepreneurs as a breed and says he sees common traits:

'Of course, there are big exceptions, but they have less formal education than you would expect; many have suffered a family incident, either a bereavement or divorce; there is a correlation of ten between the person and being good at sport; they are risk takers and they are prepared to make sacrifices – mainly, sadly, in terms of relationships or their own health. Great entrepreneurs wake up in the morning and say, "it's not working, let's change it". They don't whine or give up.'

He is at pains to stress how he does not consider himself a success. 'I'm humble. I want to be remembered as a good father, a good man, rather than anything to do with money,' he says. With mates worth £10bn, that could be tricky.

Sir Martin Sorrell

'Guard against complacency'

When talking about success in business Sorrell refers to important factors such as persistence, communication and luck. He also says:

'To be successful you need to know how to handle the difficult stuff. It's easy to make money when the tide is rising. In the 1990s you could be a success by simply walking into the office and standing up. It's not like that now. Some people have the desire to start a business. Others are passionate about growing a business but it's unusual to be both things. But that's what I've done.'

He certainly has. In 1985 Sir Martin Sorrell took a stake in Wire and Plastic Products Plc (WPP), a UK manufacturer of wire baskets. His plan was to use this public entity to build a worldwide marketing services company. In 1987 WPP acquired the J. Walter Thompson Group for $566m; it listed on the NASDAQ in 1988; it acquired The Ogilvy Group in 1989 for $864m, and the list goes on and on.

Today, WPP is one of the world's largest communications services groups. It employs 130,000-plus people, has more than 2,000 offices, operates in 106 countries and has revenues of more than £6bn. 'Luck is important in business, but you make your own luck,' says Sorrell. 'But if you are not persistent, you won't be lucky. You need to be quick, to be humble and you need to guard against complacency.'

Sorrell's father was a successful Jewish businessman, trading in electrical goods, meaning the young Martin was exposed to business and his father's businessman friends from a young age. 'I was always used to hard work,' he says. 'My father worked 24/7; he'd have sales meetings on a Sunday and was always working.' Sorrell says another big influence on his life was Sir Jules Thorn, the founder of Thorn Electrical Industries, which later became Thorn EMI. A friend of Sorrell's father, Thorn encouraged Sorrell to go to Harvard Business School. After studying economics at Cambridge University, that's exactly what he did. Sorrell says:

'Going to Harvard was an opportunity to go abroad for two years and also be exposed to the world's most powerful economy. I was the second youngest of the whole year. It was a valuable two years in my life. We did a lot of practical stuff. We looked at three case studies a day. The trouble was we all came out thinking we could run the world. We were arrogant.'

Sorrell's advice to anyone is that if you get a chance to get a formal business education, take it. He says, 'If I am hiring, I will always tend to go with the person who has a formal business education. You learn a lot about a lot of industries and businesses.'

Sorrell's love of America remains to this day:

'I love the US. I've got an affinity with the place from going to Harvard and because I have family there. People wrote off the US in the 1980s and they're doing the same today. But it's still a multi-trillion dollar economy and it's still important to us and will continue to be so.'

A recurring theme of Sorrell's, with his uniquely global outlook, is the state of the world and the scope for opportunities and potential in different areas of the world. While some talk of China and others Brazil, Sorrell will cover China, India, Brazil, Mexico, Nigeria, Indonesia, Argentina and Russia in one sentence.

He says that the secret of his success has been the free trade environment he operates in. His concern is that protectionism will creep in. He says:

'Of all the regions in the world we operate, I think the biggest dangers are in Western Europe. It needs a much more co-ordinated approach but the British will do something, France something else, Germany will hold back. While at the same time India and China are heading back to the pre-eminent position they had a few hundred years ago.'

He is a fan of China. 'I've had very few negative experiences in China,' he says. 'I love doing business out there and I find the Chinese people very welcoming.'

He notes that the British can be arrogant in their business dealings with other countries, though. 'As Britain is so small, we're by nature a trading nation. With a huge market like the US, it's little wonder American companies concentrate on its internal market. We can't do that in Britain.' But there can be problems. 'The British sometimes think they are the most creative or intellectual,' he says. 'But the reality of population size is against that. What are there, 1.1 billion, 1.5 billion Chinese? And we think our 60 million produces the best creative work on the planet? It's good in Britain, but it's not necessarily the best.'

Looking further afield, Sorrell says the future looks bright. 'Take Pakistan; even with its problems, the country is still booming. The same goes for Vietnam, for Indonesia. The next 11 BRICs [fast growing developing economies] are coming and people need to be mindful of that.' Sorrell talks excitedly about the huge opportunities that Asia, Eastern Europe, South America and Africa all offer.

In terms of his own business, Sorrell says people are motivated by a clear vision and they are also motivated by growth. But he believes it's also important to communicate internally and externally. 'No communication doesn't pay,' he adds. 'In large organisations it can be difficult. There are blocks on communication. As the person at the top, you hear about the good news quickly, but not the bad.'

Sorrell also says it is important to find yourself a sounding board, someone not too closely associated with your business, to discuss problems honestly. 'My father died in 1989,' he says. 'I used to talk with him four or five times a day, even when I was busy. He was clever, intellectual and I found it to be a great help to me.'

Sir Martin Sorrell concludes by outlining his passion for the business. 'Bill Shankly [the former Liverpool FC manager] used to say football was more important than life and death. I feel the same way about WPP.'

Peter Jones

'If you are going to dream, dream big'

Entrepreneur and *Dragons' Den* investor Peter Jones founded Phones International Group in 1998. Today, turnover is around the £150m mark and Jones himself has won a variety of awards for his entrepreneurship and business acumen. He was appointed Commander of the Order of the British Empire (CBE) in the 2009 New Year Honours. He is perhaps better known by the public for being one of the five 'Dragons' on the BBC TV show *Dragons' Den*, a hugely popular programme where wannabe business tycoons plead for investment and backing from Jones and his fellow investors. Jones joined the show in 2005 and has a variety of investments as a result, from a contemporary circus company, to i-Teddy and Reggae Reggae Sauce.

But while today he is thought to be worth more than £150m, it hasn't been all plain sailing for the Berkshire-born Jones, although he did always have visions of making it in business. 'When I was seven,' he says, 'I often went to my father's office in Windsor because I loved sitting in his big chair and pretending to be in charge of a big company, even though it was a small office and just him.'

His parents sent him to private school but he says it didn't suit him, so he left. Aged 16, after completing the Lawn Tennis Association's coaching exams, he set up his own tennis coaching school. 'This allowed me to combine the two subjects I loved the most: sport and economics,' he says.

Jones went on to run a successful computer business and own a good house, a BMW and a Porsche. But it didn't last. A combination of circumstances, personal mistakes and 'learning the hard way when a few major customers went out of business themselves', he lost the business. It taught him a valuable early lesson in business but it resulted in Jones having to move back in with his parents. Aged 28, he decided to join computer firm Siemens Nixdorf and within 12 months was running the business in the UK. Jones was the youngest-ever head of a business unit at the company.

Working at Siemens Nixdorf allowed Jones to save the money to start his own business and he founded Phones International Group in 1998. The firm 'provides mobile cellular solutions' to a broad range of clients and counts every leading brand in the mobile industry among its business partners, whether as a supplier, customer or collaborator.

Today, Jones is well used to giving advice to aspiring entrepreneurs, many of whom haven't thought through or properly researched their business idea. But for Jones, it's simple. He has 10 rules for what he calls entrepreneurial excellence. These are: vision, influence, confidence, commitment, being results-orientated, timing, perseverance, being caring, action and intuition.

Jones himself is passionate about business. He says, 'If you are going to dream, then dream big – reaching one horizon always reveals another.' When discussing confidence, he says, 'An inner self belief is like a foundation stone beneath the tallest building. There is no such thing as failure, only feedback.'

Jones says that being results-orientated is vital for successful entrepreneurs and it brings clarity to the goals for all concerned. This boils down to putting energy and focus into their business and ideas. He also says that any new business venture will require most of the founder's time, effort and dedication and that they must be ready for the sacrifices.

Finally, he says the one thing all entrepreneurs have in common and a pre-requisite for success is perseverance. 'Determination and persistence are vital for all entrepreneurs,' he says. 'Business owners need to develop a "keep on keeping on" mentality.'

Just to prove that Jones is the business brain he claims to be, he was challenged in 2008 by a national newspaper in the UK to sit a college-level business exam. He accepted the challenge and got an 'A' grade without having any background on the two-year course.

His success on *Dragons' Den* and his entrepreneurial flair led Jones to approach UK TV producer and personality Simon Cowell about developing a similar idea for US audiences. In 2006, the pair created a new business reality format show for America's largest network, ABC, called *The American Inventor*. It became a No.1 show for

ABC in America and the network's biggest success for a Thursday primetime slot in years.

Away from his phone business and TV commitments, Jones is regularly found banging the drum for growing businesses in the UK and in 2009 launched the National Enterprise Academy, a £22m joint initiative with the British Government aimed at fostering the entrepreneurial talents of the country's teenagers. The aim is for a national roll-out of regional hubs and satellite academies that will open over the next four years. Jones says:

'I am extremely passionate about this project. It has been a long held dream of mine to nurture the next generation of entre preneurial talent, particularly those who are disadvantaged in some way. Now more than ever, it is world-class enterprise education, such as that which will be provided by the National Enterprise Academy, which will ensure the future success of our economy.'

Michael Peters

'Concentrate on what you do best'

'Working with Margaret Thatcher taught me about leadership' says Michael Peters, founder and chairman of global design consultancy, Michael Peters & Partners. 'She would ask for advice from a range of people, digest what they each told her, then come out with her recommendation, whether you liked it or not. It was something I greatly admired about her.'

Peters studied graphic design and typography at the London College of Printing before winning a scholarship to study at the School of Art and Architecture at Yale in the US, where he was awarded a Masters in Fine Arts. He then worked for CBS television in New York.

'Going to the US taught me that design was a significant part of a company's activities and that big businesses need creativity to succeed,' he says. Returning to the UK, Peters realised there was no communication in design and no ergonomics in packaging, so he set himself a goal: to revolutionise the UK packaging design industry.

When he formed Michael Peters & Partners in 1970 he quickly realised he had to concentrate on what he did best – design – and bring in business managers to steer the company. The approach worked and Peters was soon working with a range of large and small organisations, including the BBC, British Airways and Unilever. 'We designed the album cover for the Rolling Stones' *Beggar's Banquet* album. It was a packaging job, after all.'

Since then, Peters has worked with many major global brands, including Aeroflot, Carling, Giorgio Armani, Powered, Johnnie Walker and Russian Standard Vodka. He was awarded the OBE in 1990 in recognition of his services to design and marketing.

He learned his approach to clients from his grandfather. 'He used to tell me to treat everyone as a friend. I feel that clients need to be bold, they need to outline their philosophy, their ideas and ambitions, and they need to put their faith in their communications people.'

He takes a similar approach to his own staff. 'Many people who work with me have done so for years and we're all partners. It doesn't matter who makes the tea. At one time I had 600 people working for me and they'd all get a handwritten birthday card.'

Peters says UK firms are increasingly adopting the US approach and appointing creative directors to their boards. And it can be the making of a company or new product.

'Look at Apple or Nokia,' he adds. 'Design is central to what they do and is a reason for their success. Of course the products are good but the design is just as impressive.'

Dr Kartar Lalvani

'Hard work and fear of failure'

Kartar Lalvani set up Vitabiotics, the UK's first specialist vitamin supplement company, in 1971. Today, the business exports to more than 100 countries, employs 2,200 people, and has factories and offices in six countries. Turnover of the business is more than $371m. He's come a long way from his birthplace in Pakistan.

Lalvani was born in Karachi, Pakistan, in 1931. His father was a successful pharmacist and times were good. But they were about to change in 1947 with the partition of India, forcing the family to flee to Bombay, where they had to start again from nothing. It was a difficult time for the family, but Lalvani says that in retrospect it was the making of him. 'Without partition, perhaps my brothers and I would not have been so entrepreneurial,' he says.' 'But because we witnessed my father losing everything, it made us determined that such a thing would not happen to us.'

Lalvani travelled to London in 1956 to study and he completed a post-graduate degree in pharmacy at King's College. He followed that with a doctorate in medical chemistry at Bonn University, finishing with a distinction.

Lalvani says his fear of failure drove him on, but it was applying himself to his studies and working all hours of the day that are the real reasons behind his extraordinary success. 'I was always overworked,' he says, 'but happily overworked. I'd work 17 hours a day but be happy doing it.'

It was a personal issue that presented Lalvani with his first move into business. As a young man, he suffered with mouth ulcers but treatments on the market didn't work for him. They might alleviate the immediate pain but not cure the problem. But by using a combination of vitamin C and powder taken from a diarrhoea tablet, Lalvani managed to successfully treat his condition. The product, called Oralcer, was to be the first for his new business Vitabiotics; the year was 1971 and it was also when the hard work started.

Getting the product into large pharmacy chains in the UK proved more difficult than he had expected. For starters, there were not many young Sikh men in London in the 1970s creating innovative new pharmaceutical products, meaning that progress was slow.

But so convinced was Lalvani that his product worked and that it would be a success that he set up his own business and he spent all his savings on patenting the product. He decided to pound the streets trying to sell the product in person to pharmacists but, by his own admission, it was a dismal failure – he only sold £5-worth. But again, the experience taught him how to handle rejection and, over time, he refined his pitching technique so that, when it came to his next product, a multivitamin called Omega H-3, he would be ready.

His first big break came selling the product via his brother's pharmaceutical business in Nigeria and the revenue meant that Vitabioitics had a future. But still he had problems raising finance. 'I've had an account with NatWest bank since 1957,' he says. 'But even after 25 years of having an account, they still wouldn't loan me money.' The impact on his business was that growth was slow. The impact on Lalvani was that he became super-focused on value for money and he was careful in terms of expansion and investment.

The global aspect of the business is now run by his son, Tej, and it's a busy period in the firm's history. It is building a new factory in Egypt, acquiring a manufacturing plant in Indonesia and looking to greatly expand its US presence. 'We look at the demographics of a country, the economic fundamentals, and generally start in a new territory by working with a distributor and going from there,' says Tej. 'If sales are strong we then think about working with local partners or going into the country ourselves.'

The company has gone on to develop one of the best treatments, again only using natural ingredients, for HIV/AIDS, and Lalvani is animated about the upcoming launch of what he says will be his best ever innovation: 'the only anti-wrinkle cream that actually works.'

Kartar Lalvani says his success is the result of hard work and study and being extra cautious when it comes to doing deals and making investments in new markets. His son Tej agrees. 'It's been too easy to borrow money but then spend it in the wrong way,' he says. 'For us, it's about negotiating better deals, asking for a better price all the time and keeping on top of all costs at all times.'

Kartar Lalvani doesn't seem to be aged 77, although he is. While he doesn't look 35, he says he feels it and there's no denying the sparkle in his eyes and his palpable enthusiasm. He is an absolute believer in his products, of course, and it has to be said that they appear to be working on him. Giving a demonstration on the new anti-wrinkle cream, Lalvani's eyes light up and even his modest demeanor seems to be struggling to keep a lid on what he can see as the potential for this new product, that has been 16 years in the making.

It's just the latest innovation for Lalvani and Vitabiotics, in a life that has seen him win numerous business and enterprise awards, in addition to the recognition his products have received from organisations such as GlaxoSmithKline and Ernst & Young. But even that's not enough.

Lalvani shows absolutely no signs of slowing down. He's just opened an Indian restaurant in London, Indali Lounge, with food based on the same scientific approach he brought to his medicines – all natural, he says, and all better for you than the usual Indian cuisine. Lalvani has even patented a new form of naan bread and he's developed new types of yogurt. Oh, and he's also found time to finish a book on India's colonial history.

If only you could bottle Kartar Lalvani.

Duncan Bannatyne

'Go for it!'

'My advice to young people is "just do it",' says serial entrepreneur Duncan Bannatyne. 'I mean, it's like going to the gym. People say they want to go but that they haven't got the time. But then they've got time to sit and watch television programmes all evening, so they've got the time to go to the gym.'

Bannatyne's incredible business career began with him buying a £450 ice cream van. At the last count, he was worth £168m, with a string of successful businesses ranging from fitness clubs to nursing homes, a casino, hotel and a new house building company. On top of that, he's a regular judge on the BBC TV show, *Dragons' Den*, has a new autobiography out and is on his way to becoming as famous as Richard Branson. 'I've been recognised three times already today and it's only 12.15pm,' he says.

Yet the fast-talking, Scottish-born entrepreneur's personal story couldn't be more different from the current crop of entrepreneurial poster boys and girls. Born in Clydebank, Glasgow, Bannatyne was one of seven children living in a two-up, two-down house. His dad worked at the local Singer sewing-machine factory; his mum, when she had time, worked as a cleaner. Though the family were not starving, money in the household was tight. Bannatyne left school with no qualifications and, aged 16, joined the British Navy.

Bannatyne doesn't strike you as the sort of man who takes kindly to authority and his Navy record is littered with minor offences, ranging from bad timing to drinking alcohol aboard ship to insubordination. His attitude problems culminated in him threatening to launch a commanding officer over the side of a boat headfirst, a move that led to him being court-martialled and found guilty of showing violence to a superior officer. He was sentenced to nine months in detention and never returned to the Navy.

Still without any qualifications and penniless again, Bannatyne had learned an important lesson in life: if he was going to achieve anything it was down to him and him only.

After buying his ice cream van Bannatyne's ice cream business, Duncan's Super Ices, soon expanded to four vans and a turnover of £300,000. From there he founded Quality Care Nursing Homes. He floated the business five years later, and sold it five years after that for £46m. For the first time ever he felt comfortably well off, but he had to decide what to do. He explains, 'it was either pay 40% tax, move to Monte Carlo for five years or reinvest the money.' He did the third, creating Bannatyne Fitness in December 1996. The firm now employs more than 1,200 people and acquired 24 health clubs from LivingWell in a deal worth £90m, bringing the number of health clubs in the Bannatyne Fitness chain to 61. Bannatyne's other interests include a hotel, a casino and bar and a housing/ property business that stretches across the UK.

But what makes him different from the many other people who set out to become successful entrepreneurs? 'A lot of people aim for qualifications, get them and get a job. And they stay in that job. That was something I aspired to when I was younger but it didn't happen for me. My attitude was if you want to do something, go and do it.' Bannatyne admits he is not the world's best manager but he copes by bringing good people in, or nurturing the talent already in the company.

'I get a lot of emails from 11 to 18-year-old kids who say they want to grow up to be entrepreneurs,' Bannatyne says. 'And that's great. I tell them to go for it.'

Edwin Booth

'Develop skills of persuasion'

Edwin Booth is the fifth generation of Booths to run the north of England-based family supermarket chain. Yet despite more than 150 years in the retail trade, Booth says that many of the challenges have remained the same. 'When it was one store, the business was up against thousands of small, independent grocery stores. Today, Booths supermarkets are up against fewer but much bigger supermarket chains, and the overall challenge is the same: to get people to shop with us.'

Booth says adaptation is the key to the longevity of a business that is set to post a turnover of £240m this year:

'Forty years ago people would shop daily and the range of produce reflected that. Today, people live much more hectic lives; they go to the gym; they eat out more, and they perhaps only shop once a week. In practical terms, it means the shelf-life of our food needs to be longer. Take bacon, for example. People simply don't have the time or inclination to eat a full English breakfast every day. In fact, you're encouraged not to do so at all. So bacon is now pre-packed and not sold in the same way it used to be.'

Edwin Booth has been chairman of the chain, started in 1847, for 11 years. But even in that time he has instigated big changes:

'We were told we couldn't do certain things, such as introduce EPOS scanning machines at the tills because we were too small. I remember kicking against that and we made the switch. Just because we're not a big supermarket chain like Sainsbury's or Tesco doesn't mean we can't be efficient and effective in everything we do.'

Yet retaining a family feel to the supermarkets, and stressing the strong history of the business, does not mean the company is not thinking like any other company.

'We maintain the culture but that's not to say the feet aren't moving quickly underneath. We employ 3,000 staff but are sympathetic to family problems or issues and let people go and deal with them while we carry on running the business. The approach creates loyalty from the staff and in fact one person left recently after working with us for 51 years.'

Booth says his senior management, as well as the family, makes a point of being out and about in the stores, talking to the customers and employees. 'I shop in our stores,' Booth says. 'But I don't turn up with a secretary in a limo.'

'One thing I've tried to do over the years is develop skills of persuasion. I've had to learn to be a chameleon, to listen to people, to really get under their skin and understand their issues.'

He adds:

'A common problem in family firms is a tendency for getting together, going on away days, endlessly talking about how everyone can get along better. But I want to run a great business, rather than be a good family business and I took steps early on to hammer that home to the company. I split the board into a family board, which deals with property, financial and appointment issues, and an operational board that looks at the key retail aspect of what we do. It's worked very well, it's a young board, but it's no worse for that.'

David Gold

'I try to embrace and encourage the people who work for me'

David Gold was born in London's East End. The secret of his success is simple: a fear of returning to the state of abject poverty he was born into:

'I'll tell you what abject poverty is. It's lying in bed every night, hungry, fully clothed but freezing cold. It's lying there next to your brother who is also freezing and hungry, and who is crying himself to sleep every night. And then Hitler came along and blew the roof off our house.'

Today, Gold is ranked 184th on the UK's Rich List, worth £450m. Gold, aged 71, made his money in adult magazines and the Ann Summers sex shop chain. His daughter, Jacqueline, runs that business (his other daughter, Vanessa, is buying director) and it currently has 153 stores with an annual turnover of £150m. Despite the wealth – he also runs Gold Air International, a jet charter company – it was only 10 years ago that he stopped having a recurring nightmare. 'It was me returning to 442 Green

Street, London,' Gold says. 'I'd still be in the Bentley but I'd have my workman tools in the back. That was one of my first jobs. The fear of that happening has always driven me on in business.'

On a practical level, Gold says it is the synergies of one business to another that have made his a success. From publishing (Gold Star Publications), to printing (he owns Broglia Press) to distribution, Gold says that controlling all aspects of his business has improved it. 'You don't want other people interfering in the chain,' he says.

In terms of his management style, Gold says he doesn't go around bullying people. 'I try to embrace and encourage the people who work for me and in return they have affection for the business. And that's good for the business.'

'I have a passion and desire to succeed, born out of my bad experiences growing up. I think determination and persistence are vital for any business. I also hate failure.' It's something he's had a taste of, having purchased Birmingham City Football Club, although sharing the highs and lows with so many fans, he says, is a unique experience and not something he gets in business.

Gold says that keeping business simple has always been the way he operates, and that he is already thinking about his own succession plan. 'By the time I retire when I'm 90, and when I'm on that beach,' he says, 'the businesses will be sustainable.'

Gold adds, 'The problem is everyone thinks they can run a business these days, but it's not easy. People ask me all the time: "how do I make a million pounds?" I tell them: start with £10m and buy a football club. You'll soon have a million pounds.'

Sir Richard Branson

'It also needs attitude, a good sense of humour'

Sir Richard Branson set up his first business, publishing a magazine called *Student*, aged 16. He then got in to music, opened a record shop called Virgin in London's Oxford Street, and soon started a recording label under the same Virgin name. He sold that business to EMI in 1992 for £1bn. Branson formed Virgin Atlantic Airways in 1984, launched Virgin Mobile in 1999 and Virgin Galactic in 2004.

Between 2000 and 2003, Virgin created three new billion-dollar companies: Virgin Blue, an airline in Australia, Virgin Mobile in the UK and Virgin Mobile in the US. In all, he's set up something like 360 businesses under the Virgin brand. The Virgin Group is estimated to have revenues of $20bn and employ 35,000 people. Some of the businesses, such as Virgin Cola, proved costly failures. But many of the others, thanks in part to Branson's impeccable knack for publicity stunts, have been huge successes. Branson regularly tops polls of most admired business people. He's enthusiastic, nearly always smiling and never wears a tie.

'There is no single prescription for running a successful entrepreneurial company,' says Branson, in his third book, *Business Stripped Bare*. 'Whether you are starting out in business or running the biggest multinational in the universe, there are some common themes that can be applied.' Branson's themes include people, the brand, delivery, learning from mistakes, innovation and leadership.

Branson initially got in to the music business in the 1970s because he spotted a gap and an opportunity. While the music being produced was cutting edge, the industry was stuck in the past. It was, he says, 'run by middle-aged guys who listened to string quartets'. So Branson decided to create a mail order record business that sold the music he liked at a discount. He secured some cut-price advertising space in a new music magazine, *Sounds*, but straightaway ran into a problem: he had no credit, no references and no records. But here's how he found a way round the problem.

He secured a deal with the magazine where he paid them a month in arrears. He got a discount on records from a shop in London, mailed them out to the public and in that way started the cash flow. After a few months, the money arrived, the magazine and record shop were paid, and the public were getting cheap records. Branson and friends achieved this by 'stuffing brown packages with cut-price Virgin mail-order albums' from a crypt under a church in Bayswater, London. That's how it all started. But they weren't making any money. It taught Branson that turnover can be huge – but more important is profit margin. From the mail order business, Branson opened a shop in London's Oxford Street and the Virgin brand was born.

Branson says he strives to keep all his businesses relatively small, at least small in feel, to get and keep an entrepreneurial atmosphere. 'I feel that small, compact companies are, generally, better run,' he says. 'This is partly because people feel more connected in smaller companies.'

Branson admits that his and Virgin's success is a result of there being good people throughout the organisation. 'Being savvy is much more important than having a formal education, 'he says. When it comes to people, his tactic is to keep them fresh. 'Teams don't last forever,' he says. 'Think of a team as being like the cast in a theatrical play. Actors who work too long together on the same show for too long grow stale. When the business lets you, shake things up a little.' He believes in promoting from within and says that money isn't the answer when it comes to motivating people. Money is important, he says, but it's feeling isolated, marginalised or ignored that is often the problem.

'In business, someone who can stay cool and calm under pressure is an asset.' Branson says an ideal business environment is one where everyone has a rough idea of what everyone else is going through. 'Banter is essential,' he says. 'Anonymous, over-formal, regimented surroundings produce mediocre results. Niggling problems either fester, or they end up on your desk. No one runs the extra mile for you.'

A crucial part of a great team of people is the leader, a role Branson relishes. 'In my view, a boss who is willing to party with all of their people – and pay attention to their personal concerns – has the makings of a great leader.'

Branson is a big fan of customer service and it's something he tries to instil in all his businesses. 'If someone has paid you for something, and it goes wrong, being cagey or defensive will kill you stone dead,' he says. 'You will never see that customer again, nor their family, nor their friends. If someone has a lousy experience at your hands, they will warn people. The knock-on effect of this destroys businesses.' It's fair to say that not all Branson's businesses produce unbridled public support, with his train company often attracting criticism from disgruntled travellers.

But when there is a crisis, Branson doesn't hide and this was proved on the evening of 23 February 2007, when a Virgin Trains service from London Euston to Glasgow Central derailed near Oxenholme in North West England, killing one lady and seriously injuring five others, including the driver. Branson, on holiday at the time, was quickly on the scene. He met the victim's family and was obviously emotional about the disaster as he faced the TV crews covering the incident. While many multinational company CEOs will hide behind PR people or managers, that's not Branson's style.

On the topic of entrepreneurship, Branson says:

'Entrepreneurship is not about putting one over on the customer. It's not about working on your own. It's not necessarily about making a lot of money and it's absolutely not about letting work take over your life. It's about turning what excites you in life into capital, so that you can do more of it and move forward with it.'

Branson isn't a fan of acquisitions or mergers, something he learned through bitter experience when buying Euro Belgian Airlines in 1996. Debilitating European regulations and high fixed costs meant that Virgin was unable to kick-start the business. So now, Branson's advice is that it's better to start your own business from scratch than to be lumbered by someone else's legacy.

And there's no sign of Branson, or Virgin, giving up on the business formation. In 2008, Branson's Virgin Healthcare announced that it would open a chain of health care clinics that would offer conventional medical care alongside homeopathic and complementary therapies.

'Business requires astute decision-making and leadership,' Branson adds. 'It requires discipline and innovation. It also needs attitude, a good sense of humour and, dare I say it, luck.'

PEOPLE

'Getting the right people in the right jobs is a lot more important than developing a strategy'

Jack Welch, former chairman and CEO, General Electric

Toni Mascolo

'Education, education, education'

Italian Toni Mascolo opened his first hairdressing salon with brother Gaetano in 1963. Today, the Toni & Guy chain has more than 230 salons in the UK, a further 175 globally, and annual turnover in excess of £175m. The business runs 27 hairdressing academies globally, which train an average of 100,000 hairdressers every year, and the organisation also extends to a chain of coffee shops and even opticians. Mascolo received an Italian knighthood in 2006 and in 2008, an OBE. In 2003, he and wife Pauline (an apprentice he met in his first salon in Clapham) established a charitable foundation that has so far raised £600,000 towards a ward within the Variety Club Children's Hospital, King's College, London. The boys from Naples have done well.

'Fantastic customer service is vital,' explains Mascolo. 'I learned very early on that you have to train your customers to come regularly for a haircut.' Another thing in the brothers' favour in the early years was their speed. 'I remember Christmas Eve 1964,' says Toni. 'I did 59 clients that day and Guy did 66. We opened at 5.30am. and didn't stop until 9.00pm. Then we had a few drinks with the girls in the shop to celebrate.' It's that sort of work ethic that set the Mascolo brothers apart. That, and bucketfulls of Italian flair and charm.

But early on the brothers, soon to be joined by their two other brothers Bruno and Anthony, spotted an opportunity. Women would go in to the salon and ask the brothers if they could cut their husbands' hair. So the Mascolos opened, what Toni claims, was the first unisex salon in the world and the business took off.

'Then we started doing a lot of shows, and we came up with product ideas, such as types of gel and mousse. We produced books of our hair styles and cuts and soon we were travelling to America, Japan, everywhere.' It was while Toni was in America that he came across the concept of franchising, something the boys applied to their business and one of the reasons for its global success. So today, the Mascolos only own 20 of the 230 UK-salons outright.

The Mascolos have worked hard on developing the Toni & Guy brand and today the company is known in more than 40 countries, from the US to China, from Barbados to Perth, Australia. It regularly receives the status of SuperBrand and CoolBrand, and it even helped Toni to get out of trouble once in Japan, as he explains:

'We were in Tokyo and completely lost. We were stuck and didn't know what to do. So we headed into the nearest hairdressing salon and I said: "I'm Toni, from Toni & Guy." The staff knew the brand and the business and looked after us from then on. It was quite remarkable.'

The company has also expanded its range of professional and commercial product lines, which are sold globally. Recognising the importance of diversification for the brand, Toni also spearheaded the development of other ventures including the Mascolo Group, which supplies all Toni & Guy salons with furniture and equipment; Mascolo Support Systems which helps all the salons with their IT requirements; and Mascolo Styles, offering vital business and financial guidance and support.

But like all Italians, it's family that is central for Toni. 'I think working with family has a lot of advantages,' Toni says. 'You work as a team, have shared responsibilities and great loyalty. But you must have clear job descriptions and you need to have set guidelines when it comes to the financial side of the business.' Toni explains why:

'We used to split the profit down the middle, Guy and I. But while I would be very economical and try to keep all the profits in the company, Guy would spend the profits. So we decided that we would put a set amount of money in the pot to grow the business and we would only keep our own profits, not split both of our profits.'

The Toni & Guy business remains family owned, but it's not just the brothers who are involved. In 1997, Toni's daughter, Sacha Mascolo-Tarbuck, and eldest son, Christian, founded essensuals hairdressing, the sister hairdressing business, which now has 64 salons worldwide. Sacha Mascolo-Tarbuck is global creative director of the Toni & Guy group and her husband, James Tarbuck (son of British comedian Jimmy), is the brains behind the creation of the hairdressing industry's only in-salon TV channel, watched by 90,000 clients each week, and the award-winning company magazine read by 360,000 clients every month.

One of Mascolo's mantras is education. 'Education, education, education,' he says. 'Now who was it who said that? It was me! It's always been very important to us and this business and we're very proud of putting something like 100,000 people through our academies worldwide.' But this expert tuition presents problems for the company. 'The trouble is people steal our staff,' Mascolo says. 'We train them to a high standard and other companies, who do not spend money on training, come in and poach them.' Mascolo seems sanguine about the situation, realising that it reflects well on the training the students are given, but it's still a source of a little irritation.

Going forward, Mascolo says 2009 is a time for opportunities – and when the best brands and products on the market will do well. And despite the success and awards, Mascolo still cuts hair in his Bond Street salon. 'Where would you rather be,' he asks 'sat in an office all week or in the salon talking to customers and meeting people? I love it.'

Sir Tom Farmer

'Look after your people. And your customers. And your suppliers'

He founded, grew and then sold his business for £1bn, was knighted in 1997, is a trustee of the Duke of Edinburgh's Award Scheme, is a previous Scottish Businessman of the Year, has shares in Hibernian Football Club and owns an island in Scotland. What then, is Sir Tom Farmer's number one piece of advice about being a business success? 'Find yourself an Anne.' Farmer is referring to his wife of 36 years. He explains:

'I know it sounds romanticised but it's true. I've always had great people around me, whether that was my family, friends and neighbours when I was growing up, or later my work colleagues. But the most important person in my life has been my wife. Throughout my life I've had no outside influences and that's enabled me to concentrate on my businesses.'

And his track record is impressive. Born in Edinburgh in 1940, Farmer is the youngest of seven siblings. His career began as an apprentice in a garage in Edinburgh:

'My first job was like an extension of my family and friends. I worked hard and the people running the business looked after you. And I did well for myself. But aged 24 there was a change in management and maybe they didn't care so much, so I decided to leave and set up my own business.'

That was in 1964 and the business was Tyres & Accessory Supplies:

'I employed friends from home, people I knew, and we were like a band of brothers. I had no capital, but I did have a good reputation as someone who worked hard and was good with customers. I decided to sell tyres at a discount; a newspaper did a small piece about this bunch of young guys running a business and people flocked to us. We all worked hard and had an obsession with customer service. We wanted to be fast and the best. People would come along just to watch us work!'

Farmer sold the business for £450,000 and 'retired' to America, but not for long. In 1971, he established the first of his Kwik-Fit tyre and exhaust centres, which grew into a £1bn business by 1999 when it was purchased by the Ford Motor Company.

'There are four lessons I've learned. One: look after your people. You must be a good leader; lead by example. I think I have been able to do that because I was always a good follower. Two: look after your suppliers. You want to be the best customer your supplier has. You must pay on time and have open and clear channels of communication with them. And remember, it's important that everyone is profiting from the business. That's you and the suppliers. If greed is your driving force, the business won't last. Look at UK department store chain Marks & Spencer. What a great reputation it has. When it was in trouble recently, no one wanted to see it go bust. That's because it's got a great reputation. Third: customers. Lots of people run coffee shops, for example, but it's those who build good relationships with their customers that do well. If you do one and two, three will come. And finally, if you do that lot, you will get to four: profits and the ability to look after your shareholders.

For all of that to occur, Farmer says you need good, but simple, systems in place, which supply regular information that can be easily digested.

Finally, he says:

'The good thing about [having the money] is that I have an ability to do something for other people. It's good for them and it's great for me to do. It makes me feel good. And you know what? I look forward to going to bed every night because I can't wait for tomorrow.'

Daniel Lee

'We're giving patients choice'

Daniel Lee is a pharmacist with a difference: he handles 1,000 prescriptions a day but never sees a patient. That's because his UK-based business, Pharmacy 2U, is a pioneering internet/mail order pharmacy.

Lee, from a family of pharmacists, took an MBA when he was aged 26 and used it to look into the major structural issues facing the prescriptions and pharmacy business in the UK. There are a staggering 650 million prescriptions made out in the UK every year. That's 650 million pieces of paper: a woefully inefficient system, particularly when you consider 70% of prescriptions are repeats. The problem Lee faced in proposing an internet-based prescriptions business was that sending medicines through the post was illegal. So for the business to work – and for Lee not to go to prison – he had to change the law. And you think you have business problems?

Lee recalls the inspection that took place shortly after the launch of the business:

'Three days after we launched we were descended upon by four inspectors. I think they came to close us down. But they looked at me and my background (working in the family pharmacy, my MBA), looked at the team I had with me, looked at our processes and the audit trail we have in place to ensure the right medicines are going to the right people, and they were impressed.'

As a result of the inspection, an amendment was made to the 1968 Medicines Act and the Royal Pharmaceutical Society of Great Britain amended its code of ethics to allow for internet and mail order pharmacy.

Lee's efforts have brought him to the attention of the government and he has been involved in developing an electronic prescriptions system that is due to be rolled out in all UK general practitioners' surgeries from the final quarter of 2009.

'The market for online prescriptions in the US is 15%. In the UK it doesn't exist, apart form what we're doing. So there is a huge opportunity. And the figure of 650 million annual prescriptions is increasing by 5% annually.' Just because the system is automated, it doesn't mean you have to be online to take advantage. Patients can call the company and the rest is done for them.

Lee says:

'My gran is 92-years-old. Every week she had to go to her GP, get a piece of paper from him and take it to a pharmacy that may or may not have the medicine she needed in stock. What we're doing is giving patients' choice. We're helping those who are chronically ill and making their lives easier by cutting out this time and effort-consuming practice.

Of course not all parties are as excited about what Lee is doing. 'Retail pharmacists see us as competition but competition is good and it's healthy. It's what this industry needs. At the end of the day, we're offering patients a choice. It's the patients who are at the heart of this.'

Lee says the success of the venture is the result of having a vision – and getting people on board the business early on who shared that vision. 'I can't do it all, so it was important to attract big hitters, offer them a stake, some equity, and for us all to drive the business forward.' Turnover for the year is £12m but as Lee says, it's early days and there's much more to come for this internet success story.

Sir Rocco Forte

'It is important to understand your own weaknesses'

'The reaction of most people when faced with difficult economic times is to cut costs,' says Sir Rocco Forte, chairman and chief executive of luxury hotel company, The Rocco Forte Collection. 'But they're not looking at the damage that might do to their product. After September 11, our American bookings fell. But rather than cut costs we looked at identifying new revenue streams and by doing so managed to grow the business by 5% year-on-year.'

Sir Rocco, knighted in December 1994 for services to the UK tourism industry, is the son of the late Lord Forte from whom he took over as CEO of the Forte Group in 1992. Now aged 63 and with the family worth an estimated £450m, Sir Rocco is perhaps also well known for his triathlon exploits. He represented Britain within his age group in the 2001, 2002, 2003 and 2007 World Triathlon Championships, and in July 2005, he took part in a gruelling Iron Man event in Austria (that's a 2.4-mile swim, 112-mile cycle ride, followed by a marathon), finishing in 11 hours and 40 minutes.

He says the trouble with many businesses is that they become complacent. 'It's easy to go after the easy business,' he says. 'But doing this will only be good for business in the short term' Sir Rocco says business owners must have a clear sense of what they want to do and be able to communicate that to the workforce. 'There must be a sensible appraisal of the financial realities because it's easy to get carried away,' he says. 'The trouble with feasibility studies is that they tend to be done when there are strong underlying economic conditions. People don't tend to consider the type of situation that we find ourselves in today.'

He says a lot of people make the mistake of going into business without having done enough research. 'It is also important to understand your own weaknesses and get people into the organisation who can compensate. The trouble with a lot of people running companies is that they hire expensive staff but micro-manage everything.'

Sir Rocco says he tries to set an example to his staff and makes a point of getting around his hotels to see them as often as possible. 'If we launch a new hotel we have a dinner for all the staff and, after I say a few words, I talk to the staff. To hear the philosophy of the business direct from me reinforces the message.'

He adds, 'I think the secret of my success is determination and never accepting the easy answer. My father was successful but he never went with the crowd, which there is a tendency to do. It's easy to say no to things.'

In terms of the triathlons, Sir Rocco says, 'They help me relax and get my mind off business. Plus they keep me fit and give me more energy. The season has just finished but I'll be back next year. I'm still training.'

Jonathan Adnams

'A clarity of purpose and a great team of people'

In 1872, the Adnams brothers, George and Ernest, bought the Sole Bay Brewery in Southwold, Suffolk, in the east of England. The story is that George realised he wasn't cut out for country life and so he left for Africa – where he was, believe it or not, 'tragically eaten by a crocodile'. Fast-forward 135 years and great-grandson, Jonathan Adnams, is now at the helm of the business and it certainly doesn't lack bite.

Even with the beer market in decline, consolidation among larger brewers and fragmentation at the local end of the market, with the proliferation of new microbreweries (there were 79 new start-ups in 2006), Adnams is bucking the trend. The firm's turnover has risen from £37m (2002) to £47m in 2007, with profits up from £3m to £4m in the same period. The company sells a range of products, is the UK agent for other beers, such as German beer Bitburger, runs two hotels in Southwold and owns 80 tenanted pubs. It imports and sells a variety of wine and is also moving into new territory by opening a chain of Cellar & Kitchen stores.

Jonathan Adnams says:

'It all comes down to having a clarity of purpose and a great team of people. I don't think us being a family-run business means we're different to any other business. All companies need to know their market, they need to connect with their customers and provide a great service. And we're no different.'

According to Adnams the firm has developed 'an open structure', meaning that people throughout the company are charged with contributing to, and helping to build, the business. With the business successful, opportunities for staff increase and Adnams is able to attract an increasingly higher quality of staff. Evidence of this comes in the hiring of Steve Sharp, former Marks & Spencer's executive director of marketing, store design and development, who joined the executive board in June.

'We invest in training for all our staff,' Adnams says, 'and although this sometimes means that people end up getting the knowledge and experience and then leaving us, that means there is an opportunity for someone else within the company to step up.'

Many of Adnams' customers are businesses, such as pubs and supermarkets, yet it is also consumer facing, so Jonathan is keen to stress the importance of the Adnams brand and says the firm's marketing is absolutely key to its success in a competitive marketplace:

'Our strapline is 'Adnams. Beer from the coast'. We use imagery and references to the coast in all of our marketing literature and it strikes a chord with consumers. For example, in our shops we sell mugs with the same images and we sell about 10,000 a month. Now that's what you call advertising that works.'

The business also excels at doing the right thing locally, which is essential for a large local employer, and it's not shy about talking up its green credentials. The company has outgrown its distribution centre in the middle of Southwold so, 'rather than build an ugly new one that uses loads of power and damages the environment, we've decided to do things a little differently. We've taken the opportunity to reduce noise and traffic in the town centre by moving to a disused gravel pit on the outskirts of Southwold.' Its roof will be lined with grass, solar panels will provide 80% of the hot water and reed beds will purify any wastewater to protect the local wildlife. It's more good news from the Suffolk-based brewer.

But what is it with the Adnams family, reed beds and wildlife? Maybe nature is taking its course.

Geeti Singh

'People can make a difference'

Geeti Singh is an Indian woman, was brought up in a commune, left school with poor results, trained to be an opera singer and is, by her own admission, unemployable. So are these really the perfect ingredients for an entrepreneurial pub owner?

It appears so.

As poster girl for the organic movement and ecologically aware in everything her business does, Geeti Singh is the owner of the world's first certified organic gastro pub, The Duke of Cambridge, which opened in December 1998 in Islington, London.

All of its meat comes from southern England; it uses seasonal fruit and vegetables and all of its 60-odd suppliers are small independent companies. On top of that, its policy on fish is approved by The Marine Conservation Society; its tea, coffee, sugar and chocolate are Fairtrade and even the electricity it uses is wind and solar generated and purchased through Good Energy. The Soil Association call Singh an 'organic hero' and she is a former winner of an Asian Women of Achievement award.

Not bad considering Singh was shot (in the foot) within two weeks of opening after two men started causing trouble in the pub, and considering she has faced her fair share of prejudice and sexism. Unperturbed, the business now employs 35 staff and has a turnover of £1.4m.

'I'm passionate about the environment and feel that as individuals, people can make a difference,' she says. 'I didn't go into it to make money, but through hard work and dedication it does. Yes, there is a degree of marketing that we do on the back of our values, but the business model is sound. It's not a gimmick.'

Singh explains that the ramifications of sourcing locally and dealing direct with farmers cuts both ways:

'Many of our suppliers have grown on the back of working with us and that's great news for us, them and society at large. They are employing more people so there is a knock-on effect. But the downside is that deliveries come in at random times; we have to order a week in advance and 60 suppliers with 60 different sets of payment terms is a headache. But it's all worth it.'

Singh set up a company board before the business even started, consisting of her entrepreneurial father, a family friend who is a lawyer and early shareholders. It's been a massive help. 'I go to them with small and big things and bounce ideas off them,' she says. 'It's also useful if people come to you and want answers to difficult questions, such as requesting pay rises or supplier issues. My answer is always, "I have to check with the board".'

She also advocates getting away from the business once or twice a year:

'I go to see my father who lives in France each year for a long weekend to talk about all facets of the business. It's always really busy and hard work to get away, but once I'm there it really enables me to be objective and think strategically about the business.'

James Caan

'An idea is nothing without good people'

James Caan is CEO of private equity firm Hamilton Bradshaw. He may be better known today as the cool, calm and steely-eyed entrepreneur/investor on the BBC TV show *Dragons' Den*. Caan founded executive head hunting firm the Alexander Mann Group in 1985, building it to a turnover of £300m with operations in 50 countries. He founded international head-hunting firm Humana International with partner Doug Bugie in 1993 and by 1999 it had 147 offices across 30 countries.

He set up London-based Hamilton Bradshaw in 2004, a private equity company specialising in buyouts, venture capital, turnarounds, investing up to £10m in each individual transaction.

Commenting on success in business, Caan says:

'To be successful in business you need to find a differential. A lot of ideas are 'me too' ideas. When I started Alexander Mann, there were four types of recruitment firms: high street, high volume agencies, mid-market firms and executive head hunters. The mid-range agencies simply put ads in papers for companies seeking middle managers, whereas the top-end firms headhunted for people on salaries of £100,000 plus. My approach was to headhunt middle managers; that simply wasn't being done. My mantra was observe the masses and do the opposite.'

Caan, a Harvard Business School graduate, says he accepted from an early stage that he couldn't do everything. He says:

'Knowing and recognising that is important. It's not a failure – it's normal. Often there is a big gap between the entrepreneur and the next best person in the organisation. I see it all the time and it is a gap that is too big. I have always tried to hire people better than me.'

Caan says the real secret to growing a successful business is to incentivise people, to give them an equity stake in a business, so if they are creating value for the business they are also creating value for themselves.

How about his mistakes? 'I make mistakes when I decide too quickly. Most entrepreneurs are at 100mph, all the time, going from one thing to the next. I find if I rush to decide, I tend to regret it.' Caan, the PricewaterhouseCoopers Entrepreneur of the Year 2003, adds that making money isn't easy. It requires planning, understanding the risk, mitigating risk and going over the financials properly.

'Too many entrepreneurs put too much emphasis on the idea and not enough on the people they will need to make it a reality. They become obsessive about the idea, whereas it is people who create success. An idea is nothing without good people.'

If he has one piece of advice for budding entrepreneurs, it is to concentrate on the execution:

'You may be launching a product which sounds great and has a great name. But the really important part is to think about the market for the product. Who will buy it, what will they pay, how will they buy it? Ideas are easy; it is the execution of an idea, of a business, that is the key to success.'

Barbara Cassani

'Spend time getting the right people on board with the right mix of skills'

Barbara Cassani came to prominence in the UK when she launched British Airways' budget airline Go Fly in 1998. She later became the first leader of London's bid for the 2012 Summer Olympics and today she is executive chairman of hotel chain Juries Inn, a business looking to expand by 30% in 2009.

Cassani says one reason she landed the Go Fly job, apart from a case of 'right place, right time', was because of her reputation for straight talking. 'Some executives might think it's a great opportunity for them to launch a new airline, fullstop,' she says. 'But the British Airways CEO knew that I'd have to persuade myself that it was a good idea before I'd get involved.' She had also bought and sold businesses during her previous 10 years at BA and had very clear ideas on how she wanted the new business to operate:

'I wanted to break down the hierarchy and ensure there was less double talk. We were very open with staff and I think that's important. We also encouraged people to try things. Everyone makes mistakes but we reacted quickly and didn't spend a lot of time pointing fingers or blaming people. I get the feeling that a lot of managers know all the jargon but don't change their behaviour.'

She says the other important aspect of her success was in picking a good team of people and 'not people who were like me'. She adds:

'You need to spend time getting the right people on board with the right mix of skills. You have to realise your own weaknesses and limitations and account for that. You certainly need to spend more time picking people than you do on things like staff uniforms or the logo.'

In 2001, Cassani led a management buyout of the company, backed by 3i, and became its first chief executive. The company was bought by easyJet the following year and the experience taught Cassani a valuable, if painful, business lesson: 'When you take other people's money, you are beholden to them.' She adds, 'I thought we had more control over the business than we did and the sale was a sobering but important lesson for me. I'm much more cautious now about putting my heart into what I do.'

Cassani advises any business leader to spend as much time as possible in their business. 'It's one thing sitting in your big office having ideas; it's something else understanding the realities of implementing the ideas. You need a sense of the people who work for you and the environment they work in,' she says. She adds that making the time to visit employees, factories, shops or offices is something that should be scheduled into senior people's diaries three months ahead. 'The first thing that usually goes into diaries are the board meetings, then the meetings ahead of the board meetings, then staff appraisals and there is often no time left to visit the people who really matter in any business – the employees.'

Her final piece of advice for anyone running a business is something everyone can do and something that is absolutely free. 'Say thanks to staff. It's easy, cheap and makes a massive difference,' she says. 'It's amazing how few business leaders do it.'

Brian Henderson

'We pay above the market rate and we're flexible with the employees'

Brian Henderson was born in Zimbabwe. He went to school at Falcon College in the south of the country and excelled in a range of sports, from water polo to hockey, from swimming to athletics. 'Because we all boarded,' he says, 'the only way to get out through the school gates was to be on a sports team, so the sporting environment was very competitive.' It is something that has stuck with him, although leaving Zimbabwe to study electronic engineering in South Africa posed a difficult problem: four minutes up the hill to college or four minutes down the hill to the sea. His studies didn't fare well.

Henderson soon returned to Harare, Zimbabwe, where he began working for IBM, but with the political situation beginning to deteriorate, in 1989 Henderson left for the UK. He worked at Reuters Healthcare for eight years doing a range of IT-related jobs. The internet was coming into its own, and with Henderson's knowledge and expertise, he decided to go it alone and he started technology firm Swebtec.

'Our first big break was when we were approached and asked to create an online property portal,' Henderson says. 'But at that stage they had no finance, no clients and no customers. So we proposed a plan to them whereby we would do the work for less cash but for shares instead.' The website Swebtec created in 2001 was Primelocation.com and it was sold to the media group Daily Mail and General Holdings in 2006 for £47m in cash. 'My only regret is not having more shares,' Henderson says.

Although the beach was beckoning again, Henderson and Swebtec used some of the funds to invest in, and create, a new piece of bespoke software aimed at the UK's 12,000 pharmacies.

Henderson says:

'We had been approached to help with a Windows-based system for the UK's pharmacies. So we did a lot of research into the area but ultimately decided against getting involved because we thought it would be a much better idea to use a web-based system. However, we did see a glaring hole in the current systems used by pharmacies and knew that the pharmacies themselves weren't necessarily happy with their providers. So, after the sale of Primelocation.com, we went back to it and developed pharmaSys.'

Currently, pharmacy software is built on technology that does not allow for good quality or speedy data flow between pharmacies and the UK's National Health Service (NHS), or for those pharmacies which are part of a large group, the pharmacies' respective head offices. That means there are efficiency problems and the data available to the big pharmaceutical firms is generally at least a month out of date. Swebtec's system, using the internet, is fast and allows all parties to see data in real time, whether for the purposes of running a one-off pharmacy or a multi-branch chain of pharmacies. The NHS has just given the product authorisation for a full UK rollout and now Henderson and his team are busy signing up pharmacies.

'Apart from spotting an opportunity and trusting our instincts to be able to create the right product,' Henderson says,' the reason we've been successful is because all the top guys here have a stake in the business. We also pay above the market rate and we're flexible with the employees.' One, a South African, wanted to return to the country for six months but he continued to be employed by Swebtec and worked from there. He's since returned to London and to the business. Swebtec's plan, to revolutionise technology used by the UK's pharmacies, is on track.

Lord Karan Bilimoria

'Lifelong learning'

For Karan Bilimoria education and lifelong learning are key elements of success in business.

Karan Bilimoria set up Cobra Beer in 1989. At the time he had £20,000 of student debt and was entering one of the most competitive beer industries in the world, with absolutely no experience. On top of that, Cobra's first shipment arrived at the start of a recession in 1990. Today, the company sells 50 million bottles of beer worldwide annually, exports to 40 countries, employs 150 people and has a turnover of more than £80m.

This stunning success has resulted in Bilimoria becoming one of Britain's youngest peers and the first ever Zoroastrian Parsi to sit in the British House of Lords. But Lord Bilimoria, of Chelsea, as he is now known, remains approachable and humble.

He puts his success down to a firmly held vision, a commitment to lifelong learning and hiring the right people. Drive and determination are a given for most successful entrepreneurs. In Bilimoria's case this was backed up by qualifying as a chartered accountant in London and graduating in law at Cambridge.

He says:

'It would be fair to say that I've spent a lot of time on my education. I started Cobra Beer in 1989 and for years I focussed intently on building my company from scratch. But in 1998 I went to Cranfield on the Business Growth Programme, and the difference was remarkable – I came back to Cobra inspired and full of new ideas.'

Lifelong learning is something Bilimoria has tried to embed in the culture at Cobra. 'I myself go on annual courses at Harvard Business School and London Business School, and everyone in the company is encouraged to go on courses and take regular training.'

Fatherly advice was another source of inspiration for Bilimoria. 'One piece of advice that will always stand out came when I was starting my first job,' explains Bilimoria.' At the time, my father said to me, "when you are given a task, the first thing is to do it. Then, do that little bit extra that you were not asked to do ". What he was saying was be innovative, be creative – always go the extra mile.'

It's something Cobra Beer makes a point of doing and you can see evidence of it from the bottles. In 2003 Bilimoria decided, almost on a whim, that the packaging required a revamp. Now, the bottles are embossed with the story of Cobra's development. It's only detail (no doubt one that caused the bottle manufacturers a headache), and of course the beer doesn't taste any different, but it shows a man who follows through on his impulses.

So the product works; sales are good. What is next for Bilimoria? He says, 'The most important aspect of business is the team. At Cobra we hire for will, not for skill - although getting both is a plus.'

Finally, Bilimoria has got himself and his company to where it is today by 'putting something back into the community'. It's the sort of platitude that sets eyes rolling, but as with many successful entrepreneurs, including Bilimoria, it's part of the company ethos.

'Despite all the challenges and hurdles,' he says, 'we had a wonderful opportunity to put back into the community. We could do it right from the very early days, donating beer, and later our wine, for charity fundraising, cultural and artistic events. It was a wonderful win-win situation, as these groups get our support as a donation in kind and we get exposure for our products.'

But it's not just blatant marketing, as Bilimoria explains, 'We launched the Cobra Foundation earlier this year to support a variety of charities. Giving back and engaging with the wider community is so important in business - it is an attitude and a way of life.'

Daniel Priestley

'We gave incentives to senior staff through stakes in the company and profits trebled'

Daniel Priestley's mum nearly burnt their Brisbane house down when he was 10 years old. As his father was about to throw out all the fire-damaged goods, Priestley asked if he could try cleaning them up and selling them in a garage sale. He then asked the neighbours if they had any rubbish he could try and sell at the sale. Not only did he make enough to buy a new computer, he got himself a brand new BMX. It was an early lesson in business. Later, he worked in McDonald's for a man who owned and operated several franchised outlets employing a lot of staff. The man became a mentor. He explained that because Priestley (like the rest of the employees) was earning $5 an hour, it meant that he, the owner, was earning $10 an hour, while not even working. That was lesson two.

One Valentine's Day, aged 18, Priestley purchased 100 red roses for $40. Dressing up in his dad's tuxedo, he sold them door-to-door for $400. Later, after enrolling in an enterprise course at college, the students were asked to come up with an imaginary business. Priestley's idea was for an alcohol-free club night for 15 to 18-year-olds. So he started doing his research for the not-real business, asking teenagers whether they would come and how much they would spend.

Priestley explains 'They all started asking, "so, when is this night?"' It dawned on him that the opportunity was real, so he called the biggest nightclub in Brisbane, spoke to the manager and, well, blagged it. The first night saw 600 students each pay $5 to get in. By the seventh time he ran the night, he was charging $15 a head and attracting 1,200 kids. He dropped out of college.

Today, Priestley is MD of Triumphant Events. The business started, and took-off, in Australia but now he's in London, attempting to repeat the success:

'It started because I heard about this entrepreneur doing a three-day course and offering his advice. It was $1,000 but I went along and it was very interesting. But more interesting was the realisation that 70 people had each paid $1,000 to sit in a room listening to this guy. That's $70,000!

He approached the firm that promoted the event and asked to work for it. It's a method he swears by, whether that's working for, or with, a company you admire. The guy took him on. 'After a year or so of seeing how it all worked, I suggested to the owner that we run regional events, rather than just in Sydney or the big cities. I told him I needed $25,000 to get it up and running.' Six months later, turnover was $280,000. He left and started his own business. Today, Triumphant Events aims to become the biggest entrepreneurial speaker business in the UK.

'My strength lay in coming up with the ideas. I'm no good with the mechanics and I'm terrible to have around in the office. I realised I was holding on too tight and everything rested with me. So I stepped back from the business in Australia, incentivised the senior staff with stakes in the company and profits trebled.'

The UK business has started well, not least due to its business plan. 'We've got 120 marketing partners,' Priestley says. 'These are people or organisations with the sort of contacts we need to come to our events. We send them an email invite to send out to their contacts, which they do for a percentage. So, rather than us cold-calling people, they are getting invites from people they know.' Of course the company promises good speakers. But the net result so far is sell-out events and a turnover of $1m (US) in just three months. Not bad for a man still in his mid-twenties.

Mike Clare

'Getting the right people and keeping them motivated is vital'

'Our delivery drivers are the last contact most people have with us, says Mike Clare, executive chairman and founder of Dreams plc, one of the UK's leading bed specialists. He continues:

'The problem is when it comes to delivering beds, the drivers are often in big dirty boots and the bedrooms most likely have a cream-coloured carpet. The drivers will have holes in their socks and the customers won't have laid any covering on the floors. So we give all our drivers branded slippers which they wear to deliver the beds. Customers can't believe it and it leaves a great impression.'

It is attention to detail like this that has seen the business expand from a single showroom in 1987 to its current portfolio of more than 150 bed superstores throughout the UK, with a turnover in excess of £160m. It has grown at an average of over 30% per annum for the last five years, but the best thing is that the business remains 100% privately owned.

In recalling the contents of a speech he made at a company event, Clare says:

'A few years ago a rumour went around I was selling the company. It was at the time of a big annual company get together and I made a speech. I said "I've got five children." Most people knew I had four and thought I was announcing a love child. "My fifth child," I said, "is Dreams'. I conceived them all, nurtured them, brought them up, look after them and wake up in the middle of the night worrying about them. I'm not about to sell any one of them".'

Clare worked his way up through the management ranks of UK retail furniture companies such as Williams, Hardy's and Perrings before starting Dreams in 1987. He felt they were overly bureaucratic and simply not entrepreneurial. His company started life selling sofa beds but switched to beds in the 1990s. 'We had a meeting one Tuesday and decided to change our emphasis,' he says. 'And we changed the name to Dreams. My accountant didn't like it because he said it didn't say what we did. But then that's why he's an accountant.' Within six months the business had sold far more beds than sofa beds and it was on course to become a success.

'Of course we've had problems; business is about problems,' Clare says. 'The 1980s crash, computer problems, staff stealing stuff, competitors super-gluing our locks, but that's business. If it was easy everyone would be doing it.' Over time, the company has finely tuned its new shop launches, he says. 'We get a site, roll out the blue carpet, fit it, have a launch party, invite the mayor and have a cake in the shape of a bed.'

Clare says Dreams has larger showrooms than its competitors and shows customers the whole range of available beds, not just the most expensive. It also collects old beds from customers and recycles them. 'We've got a bed crusher. We take out the metal and wood and it gets recycled. Customers like that.'

One big reason for the retailer's success, Clare says, is its staff:

'We've got 1,200 staff and getting the right people and keeping them motivated is vital. We try and employ positive people and avoid negative people. We look for people with common sense, the right attitude and a good personality. If they are lazy, stupid or dishonest we don't hire them.'

Clare also has an interesting approach towards interviews:

'Often, it's a gut feeling with people, but it's also obvious. Are they smiley people? Are they a laugh? I remember sitting in one interview and this guy ticked all the right boxes. But he was dull. So I asked him,' "do you know any good jokes?" He was shocked. "What sort of joke?" he said. He didn't know one.

He didn't get the job.'

Clare aims to double the size of the business over the next six years and has a simple philosophy about why his business has been a success: 'Shoes and beds. If you're not in one, you're in the other.'

PRODUCTS

'Any customer can have a car painted any colour that he wants so long as it is black'

Henry Ford, founder of the Ford Motor Company

Bill Gates

'Believe in your products'

Microsoft founder Bill Gates says the secret of his success has much to do with his mother, who sat next to a senior representative from IBM at a function many years before Microsoft started and who insisted IBM meet her son to talk about his new computer-related ideas. That and the case of the mystery car. Gates explains:

'Some time after Microsoft first started, we used to come into work and there was always this car in the car park. We used to come in early and the car was there. We'd leave late and the car was still there. It became a sort of competition with all of us trying to come in earlier and leave later, but the car was always there before us or after we left. 'Who is this wonder worker,' we all asked?'

It wasn't until months later that Gates and his co-workers realised it was a hired car that someone had forgotten to take back.

Today, Microsoft has a market capitalisation of around $230bn. Its 2008 revenues were just over $60bn and it employs around 90,000 people worldwide. In 2000, Gates stepped back from the day-to-day running of Microsoft and is now non-executive chairman of the company. And he puts most of his efforts, and a fair proportion of his personal $60bn fortune, into the Bill & Melinda Gates Foundation, one of the largest philanthropic organisations in the world.

It all started in the early 1970s with Gates and his friend Paul Allen, who would later become the Microsoft co-founder. When speaking to the BBC, Gates says:

'We became almost fanatical about using computers. A company in Seattle got a really cool computer, very expensive, but they were willing to let us use it at night, particularly if we helped them find problems. So we could go in at night and use it for free. We used to go and stay all night and read the manuals. It was a fascinating puzzle. Our sophistication went up. At first we were tinkering but then we found the source code listings for the operating system in one of the trash bins. I was actually lowered into the bin by Paul Allen.'

Gates recalls how computers used to be gigantic:

'The first mini-computers were about the fifth of a room in size. And even though they kept shrinking them, they were still only circuit boards and they were quite expensive. A $20,000 computer was the cheapest they made. Then a chip company came along, Intel, and put most of the elements on to a single chip. Now at first it wasn't very powerful but Paul [Allen] explained how quickly it would improve and we thought that was stunning.'

Gates and his colleagues soon started writing software, harnessing the power of the new chips. 'Paul relied on me in terms of hiring people and figuring out the prices and doing sales and things like that,' Gates says, 'so I was in charge. But in terms of the vision of the company, he was a central element to all of that.'

It was Gates' job to go out and get customers excited about exactly what this new technology and computer software could do for their companies. And he was good at it. Gates recalls, 'We developed fantastic relationships with our customers and in fact they were asking us to do more things for them than we could. One of our difficulties was picking between the different opportunities.'

One of the biggest step-changes for Microsoft was the introduction of Steve Ballmer. They met at Harvard but Ballmer decided to pursue a traditional career path, going on to Stanford Business School then working at Proctor & Gamble. Gates says every so often Ballmer would visit the company and the two would brainstorm, with Gates explaining how the company was overloaded and how he wasn't sure about the pricing, and one summer Gates thought that it would be a good idea to try and hire Ballmer to work for the business. While all the other people at the firm could read computer coding, the prospect of bringing a non-techy person in struck some as odd. But Gates did not think so. He understood that to really grow the business, and to allow himself and Allen to concentrate on the technology, getting the likes of Ballmer on the team could help to really expand the company. He realised Microsoft needed a mix of skills in the company. Ballmer joined in 1980.

Gates says the secret of the firm's success early on was getting people to write software on top of its MS-DOS, and later Windows, programmes. To that end it recruited thousands of people to start companies and build packages, for doctors, dentists, undertakers and engineers.

'The more software we got,' says Gates, 'the more people would buy the machine, the higher the volume, the lower the price (all the components would get cheaper), which would make it more attractive. So the IBM PC became the one that created a virtuous cycle.'

Gates says the magic wasn't so much in the deal with IBM, to run Microsoft's Windows operating system on its PCs, than in the evangelisation. Microsoft, Gates and his colleagues really believed in their products. 'We had an expansive view of what we wanted to do. Most of our competitors were poorly run. They didn't understand about going around the globe, about how to bring in people with business experience and engineering people, and put them together.' Gates, however, did understand.

In terms of his and Microsoft's success, Gates says that all the founders of the business were always frank with themselves. 'Yes we made mistakes,' he says, 'but my conservative, balance-sheet approach, meant that we learnt from our mistakes. Most of our competitors were one-product wonders. They didn't think about tools or efficiencies.'

It hasn't all been good news for the business. Accusations of anti-competitive behaviour have dogged the firm and have resulted in legal cases against the business in the EU and US, but the business continues even if Gates himself is now otherwise engaged on his philanthropic interests.

He and his wife, Melinda, have endowed the foundation with more than $28.8bn to support philanthropic initiatives in the areas of global health and learning. And Gates believes there's never been a greater need. 'Whether we're talking about advances in technology or innovations in education or disease prevention, long-term strategic interests do not disappear in an economic downturn,' he says. 'Developing the talent of our young people, addressing poverty, preventing disease is always smart, no matter what the budget outlook. We're making progress. We're on the verge of breakthroughs. We can't flinch during this downturn. We need to keep investing to keep on course for a bright future.'

Mike Jordan

'Be a specialist'

Sheikh Rashid bin Saeed Al Maktoum ruled Dubai from 1958 until 1990. His son, Sheikh Mohammed, currently rules Dubai. Adnan Khashoggi is a billionaire Saudi arms-dealer and businessman. These three men are, or have been, clients of Mike Jordan's company, Cornish Stairways.

Jordan's grandfather and father were master blacksmiths. After 'growing up in the midst of a forge,' Jordan joined the Royal Navy to become an engineer, but he later returned to the family business. He realised that however good the work, craftsmen don't make money. He took on a business degree and for his dissertation studied staircases and his research uncovered a gap. Companies existed that made staircases but none were particularly good, according to Jordan, certainly not good enough to have the good name of Jordan associated with them. A business idea was born.

Jordan's first commissions were for the business parks that were being developed around the country in the 1980s. Staircases were often the first thing you'd see on entering a building. According to Jordan, they have a wow factor, or at least they can do. They enhance the value of a building and are maintenance free. Work on business parks led on to work in private homes, then recommendations to do work in the City. Then Jordan had a lucky break on the back of his father's reputation as a blacksmith. Jordan Sr was invited to speak at the Worshipful Company of Blacksmiths in London and his son attended the event. He sat next to Richard Seifert, whose architectural company had the commission to do the NatWest Tower in London. Seifert wondered if Jordan's dad would like to design a sculpture for the lobby of the building and during their conversation Jordan saw his opportunity. Why not create a stunning staircase – something that looks impressive and has a purpose? He got the job. And once you get a job like that, people notice you.

Jordan's success led him to work with Uruguayan architect Carlos Ott on the Hilton Hotel in Dubai, which brought his staircases to the attention of the country's then ruler, Sheikh Rashid. The firm has since worked on the seven-star Burj Al Arab hotel, creating 210 feature stairways and the penthouse grand stairway, as well as staircases for the Jumeirah Beach Hotel. Jordan says, 'We have a saying that we work with the world's rich and famous, but we're very privileged to get the opportunity to work for these people. We're humble, we come from humble beginnings and we never forget that.'

Jordan says his approach differs from most other businesses in his sector:

'Most companies produce a product range and it's available in white, black or grey. That was the approach 30 years ago when we started and it still is. We go to the client and ask them, what do they want to achieve? What are they looking for? And we work to that brief.'

The brief for Adnan Khashoggi's super yacht staircase was gold, marble and plenty of it. So much so the boat had to be redesigned to take the strain.

One of the interesting aspects of Jordan's business is that virtually everything is outsourced, I just orchestrate it all,' Jordan says. He employs no one directly, gets products made where they are needed and brings in people or companies to do specific jobs or to supply specific materials. He's moved away from the builder to become much more design-focussed, something which suits Jordan and supports a lifestyle enabling him to live in Cornwall, with regular trips to the world's luxury hotspots thrown in. He uses only the best suppliers and people and has built a reputation on that. Of course the client list speaks for itself.

Tony Goodwin

'Identify a gap in the market'

Tony Goodwin has built a successful business, almost lost the lot and built it up again. Between 2001 and 2003, a combination of over-expansion, market conditions, the dotcom crash and a rogue director almost brought down his global recruitment company, Antal International. Things got so bad, he jokes, that he even had to sell his Aston Martin. But the reality at the time was deadly serious.

'Next to ill-health, I think seeing the business you've built teeter on the brink of collapse is the worst thing that can happen to you,' he says. 'I wasn't sleeping; it destroyed my confidence and the whole two years were totally disorientating.'

Goodwin admits he had opened too many offices around the world – he even had one in Almaty, Kazakhstan – something he puts down to his general outlook on life and business: he was always looking to the next project without really sorting out the job in hand. Then the dotcom bubble burst in the US, leaving his business exposed; then came September 11, and to add to his business woes, he had a very smart, Oxbridge educated 'rogue director' in his Hungary office 'siphoning off hundreds of thousands of euros' and using the money to set up a competing recruitment business.

'We had major cash flow problems as a result and it undermined my willingness to take risks,' Goodwin says. 'You have to trust people in business but the episode in Hungary had shaken my trust in people. So I did trust people, just not as much, and that meant progress was slower.'

It taught Goodwin that the set-up of the business was lopsided and he moved to create a business with a greater emphasis on franchises, lessening his risk but still expanding the company. Today, Antal International has 750 staff and 169 offices in 28 countries. But of that, only 12 offices are wholly owned and only 350 of the staff directly employed.

'A lot of young people today are obsessed by coming up with something completely new,' Goodwin says. 'But they're just re-inventing the wheel. To be a success, you need to identify a gap in the market and do it better than anyone else. Offer something different.'

One thing that has helped Goodwin is the PR coverage his business gets around the world. The business is regularly quoted on TV and in the media in China and Poland, for example, something that gives people the impression that Antal is a much bigger organisation than it is. 'Total turnover for the business is around the £30m mark, but the PR coverage is the quantity you might get if you were turning over £300m,' he says.

Goodwin says the name of the business came to him during a trip to Hungary. 'I wanted a name that appealed to an Eastern European market, not something that reeked of a Britishness, like many of the well-known UK recruitment firms, such as Michael Page or Alexander Mann. The former Hungarian president was called Anthony but in Hungarian, it's spelt "Antal ". The name stuck.'

Frederick Mulder

'Research is key'

In December 2007, Canadian Frederick Mulder sold an impression of Picasso's *Minotauromachie*, an etching made in 1935, at the New York Print Fair for more than $3m, making it the most expensive single object ever sold in the field of European printmaking between 1460 and 1960. Mulder promptly donated 75% of the proceeds to charity.

The entrepreneurial Mulder has been a private art dealer for the past 33 years and is considered a world expert. His clients include most of the major museums around the world, from the New York Metropolitan Museum and Museum of Modern Art to the British Museum in London. His turnover last year was £2.5m; he has a suite of offices at his north London home, complete with staff, and has operated his business like this for 30 years.

Mulder always had entrepreneurial flair. Growing up in rural Canada in the 1950s, he sold Christmas cards door-to-door and paid his sister to go along with him, pulling a four-wheeled wagon, so he could carry more stock. His sister says Fred used to wedge his foot in the door, although today Mulder jokingly refers to his 'early expertise in customer relations'.

Later, during a flight to the UK to continue his studies at Oxford, Mulder read a book about investments that included reference to investing in Rembrandt etchings. It stuck with him and soon after he came across a sale of etchings and took the plunge. He began to take prints back to Canada to finance his trips, got hooked by the thrill, and realised he'd found his calling.

'Although I didn't use my doctorate in philosophy directly,' he says, 'it taught me how to do research, so when it came to the prints, I always did a lot of research and knew what I was talking about.' Early on, Mulder visited a buyer from a gallery in New York who looked down his nose at the youthful print salesman. 'From then on I determined never to be arrogant to anyone, always be polite, always listen, and never be rude.'

At around that time, in the 1970s, Mulder was offered a job at the prestigious art firm Colnaghi's, a company owned by Jacob Rothschild. He turned the offer down twice, at which point Rothschild asked to meet the precocious art dealer. Mulder said he'd only take the job if his pay was linked to profits. Rothschild and Mulder worked out the terms and Mulder stayed for three years. 'But really, I don't like working for other people. Still, I had the privilege of handling wonderful objects and working with very experienced people, a great correction to my youthful exuberance. And having the name of Colnaghi's on my résumé didn't hurt.'

Mulder's philanthropic leanings were with him from an early age, when donating to church was the done thing. When he started making a lot of money in the 1970s and 1980s, he realised his money could go a long way if used the right way – specifically, if it was used in an entrepreneurial way.

Six years ago he set up The Funding Network, an organisation that helps the 'mass affluent' to donate and gives charities the opportunity to pitch for funds. With branches in the UK, Canada and South Africa, so far it's raised more than £1.5m. 'What I've given in the past has enriched me so much more than it has lightened my pocket,' he says. 'I think my business is more successful as a result, since it gives me added impetus to work hard, knowing that my money will go to a good cause. It makes working more enjoyable.'

Harry Briggs

'Be exclusive'

Harry Briggs runs Firefly Tonics with school friend Marcus Waley-Cohen. The company started trading in 2003 and shifted an impressive 43,493 bottles in year one. By the end of 2007 it was selling almost four million annually. The company's aim is 'to build a reputation as the world's healthiest, most effective natural drinks' and it's not doing too badly.

The pair got in to the health drinks sector after researching the market for a friend's dad. He wanted to import a Japanese water that claimed to cure all ills. Months of researching the market, the potential, and the products on offer eventually led to nothing as far as the water was concerned. But it had opened the two friends' eyes to a potential opportunity and they decided to do something for themselves. 'We looked up the most prominent herbalists in Britain and asked them what herbs would make an effective detox, wake up and chill out formula,' says Briggs.

Eventually the pair came across Michael McIntyre, president of the European Herbal Practitioners Association and a trustee of the Prince of Wales's Foundation for Integrated Medicine, and

Andrew Chevallier, formerly a senior lecturer in Herbal Medicine at Middlesex University, UK. The experts were keen to get involved in the business and, working as consultants, the drinks formulas started developing.

Next they had to decide on the name for the business. 'When you start out in business, developing a product, you are in a bubble. You think it is the best product the world has ever seen and that it will be front page news. Of course it isn't.' Briggs says friends were supportive face-to-face but he was looking for objective opinions so started surveying people via emails and online.

He says:

'People were a lot more brutal, but it really helped when we were thinking about the name for the drinks. We thought 'Eye' was a great name. No one else did. We then thought, "how about we call it Marcus and Harry's?" People said it sounded like a couple of posh blokes. But everyone liked Firefly so it stuck.'

Their big break was their first break: getting into upmarket UK department Harvey Nichols. Briggs says, 'Harvey Nichol's wanted an exclusive six-month deal to stock the drinks but we managed to agree on one month, as we really needed to shift a lot of bottles, according to our business plan.' From that initial order, the orders started coming in thick and fast. We got a call from the buyer from Collette, the Parisian department store. She had been in London, looking at what Harvey Nichols was selling and ordered on the strength of that. A lot of buyers do that, apparently." Firefly now lists the bank Coutts, department store Selfridges, the Hilton Tokyo and the Burj Al Arab as customers, but it has turned a few down.

'Harvey Nichols don't want to go out and see the drink being stocked at half the price in cheaper supermarkets, so we don't stock in those places,' Briggs says. It's exclusivity like that which has made the company what it is.

Joy Nichols

'Reputations matter'

Joy Nichols, an entrepreneurial role model who built a successful business on her reputation, says:

'The Caribbean community was invited over to England to work for English companies. The African community mostly came to get an education. So at no point did either of these two sets of people learn to be entrepreneurial and at no point were they encouraged to start their own businesses. I did start my own business, and now I am something of a role model I suppose, which is fine, but it says a lot to me. The fact that I am a role model just goes to show how few black people run their own businesses in the UK. I want that to change.'

Joy Nichols MBE is chief executive of the Nichols Agency, a London-based employment agency. She wants the UK to be like the US: a place where people walk into a business and are not surprised to learn that a black person runs it. That's an event that is perhaps some way off.

The Nichols Agency has evolved into a three-part business: recruitment, training and consultancy. It has offices in London and

Johannesburg (more on that later), employs 15 core staff and has placed thousands of staff since its inception in 1980. The business simply evolved, Nichols explains. She worked as a secretary, something she enjoyed and was very good at, and suddenly she found herself in demand. 'I did something that I tell all my staff never to do,' Nichols says. 'I told the employer's clients that if they wanted me to work for them, contact me direct. And they did. In fact so many did that I had to start finding friends to fill the temporary vacancies and it went from there.' Nichols realised there was a business to be had: a business built on her reputation.

She was canny with the type of clients she dealt with. 'In the beginning I placed a lot of people at the Greater London Council,' she says. 'When it came to an end, most of the senior staff took up new public sector positions in the 33 London boroughs.' The clients took Nichols' staff with them and the business grew and grew. Although not exactly recession-proof, it did mean Nichols's agency was able to ride out a couple of major economic downturns.

In November 2001, Nichols launched the second strand of her business, Nichols Training. With clients wanting and expecting a temp to come in and 'hit the ground running' she realised that training was key. It meant the staff were prepared for the work and established Nichols' reputation in the field of recruitment and, crucially, in the eyes of her clients. She is also developing a consultancy arm to help small firms get to grips with how to deal with the public sector and win public sector contracts. But she's not finished there either. Nichols says, 'I was invited to Johannesburg a few years ago and realised the people there had the same problems. The jobs were there but the people were lacking the skills', something Nichols is attempting to help sort out. Although a personal mission, her efforts have brought her national prominence. She's making her second appearance at Buckingham Palace at the end of the year to collect an MBE (she was awarded a special Queen's Award in 2005 which honours 'outstanding individuals who inspire, encourage and help budding entrepreneurs.')

'I go into schools in London and talk to the kids. I feel like Daniel walking into the lions. They're spoon-fed all this easy-street rubbish, where money and bling come easy, but that's simply not reality. So I tell the kids my story: how I started with nothing but have made something of myself and they lap it up. You can really inspire them.'

Mike Lynch

'Offer something better than what is already there'

Mike Lynch founded UK-based software firm Autonomy in 1996. Its latest results show the highest revenues and profits in the firm's history. In 2008 the full year revenues were up 47% to $503.2m, while profit rose by 91% to a record $207.5m.

Lynch studied engineering at Cambridge University and obtained a PhD in mathematical computing. He has held a number of advisory and board roles in the venture capital industry and is currently a non-executive director of Isabel Healthcare. He has been named the Confederation of British Industry's Entrepreneur of the Year and was awarded an OBE for Services to Enterprise. From 2007 he has been a non-executive director of the BBC.

His advice about setting up and running a small firm is simple and concise. 'Don't bother starting a business unless you are offering something better than what is already there,' Lynch says. He adds:

'It is better to wait for a good idea. I once worked on software for synthesisers but there's people out there willing to do that sort of thing as a labour of love – plus you don't get a credit on any albums. Focus is vital: each day write down the five things to do and do them (and think about what matters most).'

'If the two founders of a company spend the first three months working out their employment contracts, don't bother, the business will never work. It is important to manage negativity, especially at the beginning when people queue up to tell you what a bad idea it is and that it will never work. I don't know if it is a British thing but I once read a great article called "10 ways to shoot down a good idea" and that attitude is pervasive.'

'When I started, people would say to me "there is no point" as if there was anything to our products, Microsoft would already be doing it. Now look at us. In the beginning, naivety saves you. I had no business experience and that helped me a lot. Another thing I do is have 'positive' and 'negative' meetings. In one we only talk about the upside of doing something or a new product. At the other we only talk about the negatives. They're very informative although if I'm honest I prefer the positive meetings.'

'To get ahead in business you need a deranged faith in yourself – although it's best not to be actually deranged. At the end of it all, will people part with their money for your stuff. If they do, it works. If not, it won't.'

'Finally, one universal truth is get good people and hang on to them. Don't bother with headhunters, find them through people you know or meet. You want to keep enthusiastic people with you. Don't get in a specialist to help grow an SME. People in SMEs need to be good at many things. Go for good people, full stop.'

Paul Tustain

'Don't be a wishful thinker in business'

Paul Tustain runs BullionVault, an online business that provides retail access to professional market gold bullion services at wholesale prices. It sells and trades gold online, enabling people to bypass gold dealers and buy direct from the market. It uses 'Betfair' technology, meaning it brings people together online to trade their gold with each other. BullionVault takes a 0.8% commission – which doesn't sound much until you realise the business turns over £2m per month, per staff member (there are eight staff). And because the whole thing is computerised, the business makes money when the staff are not even at work, with people from around the world trading gold with each other day and night, seven days a week.

Tustain's bridge partner is the brain behind Betfair and Tustain was an early investor in that business. He later ran another company, which devised software that provides real-time settlement for a range of UK and international shares, UK government bonds and other corporate securities. His present business came about when Tustain was looking to invest some money in three gold bars. It turned out to be very difficult and Tustain spotted an opportunity, especially in a time of dubious financial dealings by the major banks and government's alike. Gold, Tustain figured, was the ultimate safe bet.

One of the first things Tustain did was launch www.galmarley.com, a free educational resource for researchers seeking information on gold's monetary history, its modern role, and how it is traded around the world. It was a clever way of tapping into the potential gold-buying market.

In March 2005, Tustain raised £2m, against his house, to finance the gold bullion inventory that the business needed to operate. It enabled the business to acquire the 'float' of gold bars that are at the heart of the way BullionVault works. Today, is has customers from 85 countries and between them they own approximately $500 in stored bullion.

Tustain says there are some simple reasons behind his company's success to date, not least that no one else is offering this service. Also, the business is based on software that Tustain owns, meaning that any new entrants to the market would face enormous upfront costs.

Another positive about the business is that it's been built to scale. Tustain says his knowledge of the internet and the technology he is using means they could increase demand dramatically whenever they want. 'What we don't want to do is enter new markets, such as the US, and not be able to cope with demand, so we are taking things slowly and making the right investments so that when we do launch in the US we're ready for it.'

He adds:

'I think a lot of people are wishful thinkers when it comes to business. They think they've had a good idea. But what's stopping someone else coming in and doing it too? What are the barriers to entry? What's to say someone couldn't come in and do it cheaper than you? We don't have that problem.'

Richard Reed

'Stick to your principles'

'We've had to postpone the launch of a new product because we are struggling to find enough high-quality blueberries,' says Richard Reed, co-founder of innocent drinks.' Because, of course, fruit is finite. 'We are close to nature in what we sell and are dependent on it, which is a good thing, so we're happy to have that problem. Another issue we're facing this year is in terms of mangoes. We need twice as many as we did last year.'

The smoothie drinks business, launched from a west London industrial estate in 1999, has gone from strength to strength. The number of employees has increased from three to 200-plus; market share has risen to 65%; the drinks are now stocked in more than 7,000 outlets and the firm shifts an incredible two million units a week. It's gone from zero to a turnover of £100m-plus. All of which is pretty good going for three university friends who started out with absolutely no experience in retail, distribution – or smoothies.

Reed comments:

'The industry told us we had to use preservatives and to do otherwise would be madness, not least because the profit margins would be too small and it would lead to a shorter lifespan of the drinks on shelves. In a way I think our naivety was one of our strengths early on.'

Their 6.5% profit margin could certainly be higher but their customer base is loyal because of the firm's insistence on 100% natural products. The boys ignored conventional wisdom and stuck to their original aims – to produce tasty drinks that were good for you and that were completely natural. It's not the only area they have chosen to do their own way.

'We've never had a board meeting in seven years and I don't see the point, for us, of non-executives,' says Reed. 'I think I learn as much about the business from a retailer who sells our drinks as I would from someone coming in to see us once a month.' The lack of outside interference has allowed the business to stick to its guns – remaining socially conscious as well as financially savvy. 'We're weirdly obsessed by fruit,' Reed says. 'As a result our drinks are more expensive than others – but they are better.' Despite the relatively high prices for drinks (£1.99 for a 250 ml bottle of smoothie), the firm continues to grow.

Reed says one of the hardest aspects of the firm's growth is employing enough of the right kind of staff to keep up with the expansion:

'There are two options. Either hire staff that aren't as good, who aren't as socially conscious or financially astute as we want them to be, or ask our current staff to bear with us, work harder, and be patient. We will hire more people but they've got to be the right people.'

Staff at its London Head Quarters, Fruit Towers, seem happy to oblige.

So have they been a success? 'No,' says Reed emphatically. 'We're at the beginning, not the end. At the start we had aspirations of being a £10m-turnover business and I hoped we might one day become a truly globally, ethical company. We're going in the right direction but we could be much better.' That's not for want of trying. The Innocent Foundation ensures 10% of profits goes back into the farming communities that provide fruit for the drinks – meaning there are 18 projects in three continents funded by innocent drinks.

Efforts like that drive the founders, motivate the staff and go down well with the ethically conscious, smoothie-buying public.

Robert Hurst

'Have a long tail'

Robert Hurst used to work at Boosey & Hawkes, the largest specialist classical music publishing company in the world. It owns a catalogue of music copyrights including the works of Stravinsky, Bartók, Copland, Britten, Prokofieff, Strauss and Rachmaninoff. As someone who specialised in rights issues, he was familiar with the problems faced by companies wishing to use such music and thought that there must be a simpler way. In 2001, Hurst, and fellow Boosey employee Andrew Sunnucks decided to go it alone and fill a niche.

Hurst says:

'We left our jobs in June 2001. We spoke to a number of venture capitalists and were on the verge of doing a deal. On September 10, 2001, we had a solid offer from one. There were a couple of things we weren't happy with so wrote back to them. We all know what happened on September 11. After that, the venture capitalist pulled out. If we were on the verge of World War Three, they said, it probably wasn't the time to be investing £2m in a music rights business.'

This left Hurst and Sunnucks in a difficult situation.

The idea for Hurst's business, Audio Networks, was to pay composers to come up with a huge library of songs and sound effects that TV programmes, production companies and the public could use without fear of infringing copyrights. Hurst explained to the composers what had happened regarding funding, but they remained convinced it was a good idea. So rather than paying the composers to write the music, Hurst wondered whether they would be interested in taking a share of the business in return for their work. They agreed. Although these shares were tiny at the time, some are now worth in the region of £200,000.

But they still required funding to grow the business. 'We probably saw about 100 potential investors, in the music industry as well as professional investors,' Hurst says. 'But without a massive back catalogue there were no assets. Without the investment we couldn't grow the back catalogue.'

John Dankworth came to the rescue. His career spans more than 50 years as a performer, composer and conductor, and he's worked in a wide range of musical activities. He agreed to invest if others would join him. It was enough to get the ball rolling. British singer Cleo Laine, Dankworth's wife, was among other investors and another important big name to have on board.

Today, Audio Networks has up to 12,000 tracks and 50,000 sound effects. It works with all the major British TV companies and gets hits from across the world (including the Congo, Hurst says). It's cheap, easy to use and hassle-free.

'The cash flow going forward is lovely,' Hurst says. 'We get a tiny fee for the track, then a royalty when it is used.' The fees are cheap but it is volume that makes the money. Hosting the music is virtually free but it can sell a hundred times. Plus the royalties keep coming. On this topic, Hurst swears by a book by the former editor of *Wired* magazine, Chris Anderson, called *The Long Tail*. It is, according to the quote from Google CEO Eric Schmidt on the book cover, a brilliant book about the future of business.

Two areas of growth Hurst sees for the business are supplying music for corporate films made in-house – and YouTube. With up to 80,000 videos being posted on the site every day, the videos need music (that won't infringe copyright), which is where Audio Networks comes in. It's a business that sounds good in more ways than one.

Thomas Althoff

'Consistency is critical'

German-born Thomas Althoff runs a chain of luxury hotels in Germany, St Tropez and now London. Born in Wuppertal in 1953, Althoff became general manager of an 80-bedroom hotel in the city of Aachen aged just 21. He went on to become managing director of Best Western Hotels before, in 1988, founding the Althoff Hotel Collection.

For Althoff, the business relies on the hiring and training of good staff. And with 1,100 staff working under him, it's a big task. Today, the company has set processes in place and a clear idea of what it is looking for when recruiting – namely, quality people with as much experience as possible. But earlier on in his career, he admits that intuition played a part.

Speaking through an interpreter, Althoff admits:

'Not all the people I have hired over the years have been the right people, but I always thought I had a good feeling for people and that has improved as I have got older. It is one of the greatest challenges we face but you have to believe in yourself and trust your own judgement.'

With the hotel industry's reputation for a high turnover of staff, Althoff says training all levels of staff plays an important role in retaining people.

In 1984 Althoff and his wife, Elke, took over the management contract for the Hotel Regent International in Cologne. He says the difference between running large organisations and running your own business can be seen in the type of work you do day to day. 'Working at Best Western, for example, you are not personally responsible for everything that happens. You become more of an administrator. With my own hotels, I certainly am responsible. Running big companies you become more of a manager than a hotelier.'

As for working with his wife, Althoff says it is important to split responsibilities and competences. Elke, for example, runs the spa side of the business, and Althoff, smiling at this point, says he doesn't interfere.

Althoff says giving advice to others about running a successful business isn't easy. 'What is important for any business is consistency. It is important in the hotels business. But I also think all companies should have plans in place for the future. We have a three-month plan, a one-year, three-year, five-year, 10-year, even a 20-year plan for our business.'

He says the secret to his success is having '360 degrees vision' and one that is communicated clearly to all relevant parts of the business, from the staff to investors and to customers.

Since 2001, the Althoff Residences were added to the portfolio as a second pillar of the business, and this year the Althoff Hotel Collection takes over the management of the new five-star boutique hotel St. James's Hotel and Club in London. Althoff, a former Hotelier of the Year, adds, 'The hotel industry is very competitive so we rely on our good reputation and having a long-terms perspective about where we want to be.'

Vimal Ruia

'It is important to get the right business model'

Vimal Ruia, his three brothers and cousin are all second generation in the family textile business, the Ruia Group. His father and uncles began importing loomstate fabric to the UK from India in the 1950s. This was then dyed and sold on. It was a good business model for 25 years, says Ruia, but then the firm began importing the finished articles instead, ranging from bedspreads to slinky stockings. But with the internet, communications and the ability to travel making importing easier, the challenge for the business today is protecting what it's got. It is doing this partly by developing a range of licensing agreements with fashion brands such as Pringle, Elle and Farah and they have just stepped into the world of e-tailing with websites SockShop.co.uk and elinens.co.uk. Based at Kearsley Mill, a 240,000sq ft Victorian mill near Manchester, the group employs several hundred staff and turnover is in excess of £40m.

Ruia says trading is in the blood. 'My father came to the UK from Mumbai, India. For him and my uncles, importing goods from India was simple and it gave the business a strong start.' But when the second generation started getting involved, in the 1980s, it wasn't easy. 'I started in 1982,' Ruia says, 'and my father retired from the business in 1987. I think we had different ideas about how the business should be run.' Today, the business ensures each family director is running their own part of the business and not stepping on each other's toes. 'We're all independent people,' Ruia says, 'and we all have absolute confidence in each other's ability. It's just that we could not share the same office.'

For Ruia, the secret of running a good business is having a product or service, something unique, different, sustainable and with potential for growth. 'It is important to get the right business model,' he says. 'All your time and money initially should go into making sure the product or service is right, that it works and is continually improving. Then worry about marketing and PR.'

Ruia says it is important to get involved and acquainted at every level when working with overseas manufacturers or suppliers and he regularly gets on a plane and visits. 'Communications make overseas trade 90% easier than it was 30 years ago,' he says. 'But to do business, it must be face to face.' His advice is go to trade fairs and, crucially, get yourself an agent who can deal with the factory directly on your behalf – and who can remain on the ground when you get home.

Leading by example is Ruia's work ethic, something the current crop of directors all do, with all members of the team encouraged to take decisions. 'I think it's good to make mistakes because it's the only way you can learn and make sure things are even better for next time.'

When it comes to customer service, Ruia admits to being confused:

'If you haven't got good customer service or it's something you need to work on, you're not in the game. Good customer service is a bare minimum these days. We won an award because after someone ordered one of our products from SockShop.co.uk, it was packaged and delivered the next day. But that's normal business, isn't it?'

Charlie Bigham

'We stick to our principles in terms of ensuring the food is fresh and hand-prepared'

Bigham's employs 200 staff at its 35,000 sq ft Park Royal base in north west London. Turnover for the fresh meals business is around £14m but founder Charlie Bigham says the business is nowhere near the end. In fact, after almost 11 years running the company, Bigham says it feels as if they've only just begun.

In talking about his reasons for setting up a business, Bigham says:

'I always wanted to set up and grow a business and I think it suits my temperament. I've got pretty strong views on things which would make me a poor employee. At the start, I didn't think it really mattered what the business was, but now I realise that it's great to do something you love, particularly when things aren't going so well.

Not that the business isn't going great: it estimates that 100,000 people eat one of Bigham's freshly-made portions of food every day in the UK. Bigham explains:

'We've done well because we stick to our principles in terms of ensuring the food is fresh and hand-prepared. We get tempted all the time to include additives or introduce machines and, of course, we could make the food last longer and cost less. People say: "do your customers really care?" Well the answer is "yes they do".'

Bigham understands his customers because the firm's phone number is on the back of the packaging and customers are encouraged to ring in. In fact, customers are welcome to go and have a look round the kitchens to see for themselves that the food is hand-prepared.

Bigham has a former Marks & Spencer (M&S) employee, one of the UK's largest department stores, now working for him. He told Bigham that M&S couldn't believe Bigham's claim of responding to all customer calls and emails, so tested it. Within an hour, M&S got a response – they was astounded. 'They must have got us on a good day to get a response within an hour,' Bigham says, 'but we do strive to do what we say.' It equates to customer loyalty: one emailed Bigham to say he has bought one of the company's meals every week for the past seven and a half years.

Bigham says he gets involved with a 'disproportionate amount of recruitment' but that it is important for him and the business that people are passionate about the company and its ethos. 'I employ on attitude,' he says. 'My philosophy is that if you're proud of what you do, you enjoy it and do a better job. I've been around in this industry for nearly 11 years now and some firms don't treat their staff well or with respect.' Bigham's has a café with free internet access on site and Bigham says staff often come in early and leave late because of the good working environment.

So who does he turn to for advice? 'My motto is listen to everyone and follow no one's advice. There are experts everywhere you turn in this industry but you have to listen, filter and do what you think is right.'

FINANCE

'Being the richest man in the cemetery doesn't matter to me. Going to bed at night saying we've done something wonderful, that's what matters to me'

Steve Jobs, chairman and CEO, Apple

Sir David Tang

'A business is only a success if it is sustainable'

With some people, it's difficult to know where to start. In entrepreneur David Tang's case, it's hard to know where to stop. Born in Hong Kong and educated there, as well as in London and Beijing, Tang has a degree in philosophy, is an OBE in Britain and was awarded the *Chevalier de L'Ordre des Arts et des Lettres* in France. He has worked as a lecturer at Peking University, as a solicitor in Hong Kong and London, as well as spending time at Swires in Hong Kong and Cluff Oil in London and Hong Kong. He is a currently director, chairman or founder of 15 companies and is on six advisory boards, ranging from Asprey and Garrard in London to Tommy Hilfiger Inc. in the US. He is involved with 24 charities around the world, plays piano with the Hong Kong Philharmonic Orchestra and, for good measure, has translated Roald Dahl's book *Charlie and the Chocolate Factory* into Chinese.

Tang says his passion for food and eating led him to launch his first China Club in Hong Kong some 15 years ago. He wanted to 'bring back a bit of Chinese romance'. He also says luck was on his side, as events in Hong Kong were coming to a constitutional head with the handover of Hong Kong to China in 1997. The club filled a niche. A sort of 'East meets West' affair, where good food was served to a wealthy, and mixed, clientele. It soon became the place to be, but starting it wasn't easy. 'It was an entirely new area for me and I admit I wasn't confident,' says Tang. But after persuading people to back him (Barings Bank put in a million dollars; Tang, it's safe to say, is persuasive), Tang realised this business was like any other. 'Everything was simple. You had to concentrate on the Holy Trinity: profit and loss; balance sheet; and cash flow. If the cash flow is right, the business is right.' From then to now, Tang's view hasn't changed: cash flow is king.

But Tang didn't stop at food. He then moved into selling cigars. Tang loves cigars. He explains:

'Two men had the sole rights to sell Cuban cigars in Asia. But they only had a couple of shops and I thought it could be done much better. They were just selling cigars, but I knew it was all about selling a lifestyle. So I went to see them and asked them if they would like me to buy them out. Well, they threw me down the stairs. So I decided to go to Cuba and persuade the owners to sell me the rights. To my amazement, they did and I got a 10-year franchise to sell Cuban cigars in Asia.'

Rather than a shop, Tang set up Cuban cigar smoking clubs and they were a success. One, a 300 sq ft room, turns over $3m annually. He is now chairman of the Pacific Cigar Co. which controls the Cuban cigar franchise for Canada and the whole Asia/Pacific region.

But he wasn't finished there either. Next he developed Shanghai Tang, 'the first global Chinese lifestyle brand revitalising Chinese designs'. His chain of shops reaches from China to New York and, again, Tang has managed to ride the wave of increasing interest in China. To him, though, it's all about global brands. 'I won't do anything that can't be global,' he says. 'It's got to achieve critical mass.'

Tang dismisses talk that the Chinese are somehow particularly gifted or inherently global in their business dealings. Actually, he compares the Chinese to refugee Jews. Both, Tang says, make a success of themselves on the back of adversity. 'The 20th century saw so much happen in China. Every decade there was something else: a war with Japan, the Second World War and the Cultural Revolution for example. All those events truncated into a century, when most countries haven't experienced half of it in their entire histories.'

The quick fire history lesson over, Tang smiles and continues to puff on his enormous cigar. 'To me,' he says, 'a business is only a success if it is sustainable. So in terms of my businesses, we will only know if they are a success when I am dead.'

Corinne Vigreux

'We work hard to employ entrepreneurial people'

'I was shocked at the Christmas party this year,' says French-born Corinne Vigreux, managing director at navigation software firm TomTom. 'There were so many people there I was speechless, and that doesn't happen very often to me. It was amazing.' Vigreux is right to pinch herself. Joining the start-up in 1994, she became its third staff member and she took a 25% stake of the business. It is now the market leader in portable navigation devices, publicly listed (in Amsterdam) in 2005, had revenues of €1,364 million in 2006, is active in 25 countries, has 17 offices worldwide and now employs more than 800 people.

'I thought it was a good idea,' she says. 'And rather than I icence the software, I thought why not put it in a box and sell it through Dixons? Everyone thought we were mad but it felt right.' From 1987 until 1993 Vigreux worked for Psion Plc helping to set up and manage the firm's European distribution network. By the time she left she was international sales manager and it was experience she put to good use.

Vigreux says:

'We had belief. We were entrepreneurial and we took a risk. But we didn't sit around analysing ourselves. We understood that it was something new for people and I suppose that was one of our biggest challenges – explaining a completely new product to consumers. We created an entirely new market. In fact, some of the major retailers in Europe were sceptical at first, but they saw the potential in a new revenue stream so were willing to trust us.'

The initial order was for 100,000 TomTom devices; they sold out in three months.

One major reason for the company's success, according to Vigreux, is in getting the right people involved from the start. 'We have always set out to employ the best people,' she says. 'People better than us; I think that's important. People should not be frightened of employing people better than themselves.'

It was Peter-Frans Pauwels and Pieter Geelen, both graduates from Amsterdam University, who in 1991 started to develop applications for the first generation of handheld computers. After Vigreux joined, the company acquired the talents of Harold Goddijn, the former CEO of Psion in 2001. Two years later it convinced Mark Gretton, the former CTO of Psion and creator of the original Psion Series 3, to join. This team have built the TomTom brand into what it is today, but the rapid growth hasn't always been easy: being market leader brings with it its own difficulties. 'We have a lot of people attacking us, and now some big players,' says Vigreux. 'But we intend to retain our position as market leader and keep our entrepreneurial spirit.' The company has managed to retain all the original people involved with the business and that certainly helps.

'We're constantly running and you hope everyone is running with you,' Vigreux says. 'But sometimes you look over your shoulder and people are dropping off. So you have to account for that and get the right people in the right jobs. We're only as good as our managers, so we work hard to employ entrepreneurial people who can handle the pace.' But it's not all work.

'It's still very exciting and we're all having fun,' she adds. 'That's what it's all about.'

Edward Green

'We were able to show...there is real growth potential'

Green Biologics, a UK-based industrial biotechnology company developing 'next generation' biofuels, has just raised £1.58m. It is the third lot of funding that the company's founder, CEO Edward Green, has raised but it won't be the last. The background to all the funding is ambitious EU and UK CO_2 emissions targets. The European Commission has proposed that biofuels should make up 10% of total fuel sales by 2020. Within the UK, the Renewable Transport Fuel Obligation will, from April 2008, require fuel suppliers to ensure that 10% of their total fuel sales are made up of biofuels, rising to 25% by 2020.

'I'd say it is more difficult to raise smaller amounts of money,' says Green. 'We got our first funding, £50,000, from friends and family but they were taking a greater risk because at that stage it was just my ideas.' But it was enough to get some space at a technology incubator facility in Oxford, Subsequent funding secured £550,000 and then the latest amount, of £1.58m, was raised from existing shareholders as well as new investors, Carbon Trust Investments and Oxford Capital Partners.

'It's a little bit chicken and egg with the funding,' Green says. 'You need to show potential investors that you have a good team behind the business, but you can only afford good people when you get the funding.' Green squared the circle by entering and winning a technology competition.

Green says:

'One of the judges that day was Dr Andrew Rickman OBE, a well-respected man in the sector and an out-and-out salesman. It took a few months of talking with him but I eventually persuaded him to come on board and he became our chairman. That made a massive difference to subsequent funding rounds.'

'I think the fact that the technology is in an attractive sector helped us secure funding. But we're also product-focussed rather than simply looking to license an idea, which is also strong. We were also able to show that people are already interested in what we are doing here and that there is real growth potential.'

For the record, Green's ButafuelTM, is based on an alcohol called butanol, produced by a naturally occurring microbe in a sugar fermentation process. The company says the current 'first generation' biofuels such as bio-ethanol and bio-diesel have their limitations and that his product 'ultimately has the potential to completely replace fossil fuels for road and air transport.' It's a huge ambition.

Basing Green Biologics in Oxford has been central to the success so far. 'Along with London and Cambridge, the area is a well known for being a technology and innovation hub and, through the region's accountants, bankers and consultants, there is a lot of good advice about raising money out there; much of it free in the first instance.'

The company is now expanding to China, and has appointed Intelligent Sensor Systems as its commercial representative in China to support its business in exploiting the rapidly expanding commercial opportunities for its technology and services to Chinese bio-chemical and bio-fuel producers.

Sir Stelios Haji-Ioannou

'Cash is king'

Sir Stelios Haji-Ioannou founded easyJet when he was 28. Today, it operates 157 aircraft on 392 routes between 101 airports in 26 countries. In the past 12 months the firm has carried more than 40 million passengers. But Stelios, as he prefers to be known, didn't stop there. He has since established more than 17 ventures, all with the 'easy' prefix.

For example, the easyCar business operates in more than 2,400 locations in over 60 countries; easyBus began operating in July 2004 and currently offers a low cost express minibus service between Gatwick, Luton and Stansted Airports to Central London; and his easyCruise business, a no-frills cruise ship targeting the 18 to 40 age group, operates in the Mediterranean and now the Caribbean.

In fact, think 'easy' and you're thinking cheap, cheerful – and bright orange. To be fair to Stelios, he's not pretending to be anything else, and he admits that the initial idea of requiring easyCruise customers to be responsible for all room cleaning or incur a penalty charge 'didn't go down too well'.

But despite the basic offerings, most of his businesses have thrived and he is one of the UK's best-known entrepreneurs – odd, since he is Cypriot. With his father a successful shipping magnate, Stelios is the first to admit that his is no classic rags to riches story of entrepreneurship. But while he talks about 'luck', there's a bit more to it than that. The branding is in-your-face; the service acceptable; the price cheap – and the legal protection of the 'easy' brand vigorous.

The easy.com website even carries a specific page, entitled 'brand thieves', outlining the seriousness of attempting to copy the 'easy' brand. 'Some people think they can make a fast buck by stealing our name and our reputation,' it says. It then advises the following: 'If you see a company that you think is disguising itself as an easyGroup company or that is trying to piggyback off our brand in any way, then please help us to protect both the consumer and our brand.' You have been warned! But it just goes to show how well-known the brand has become and the importance of protecting it. It is a cornerstone of the group's success to date and the company makes regular court appearances to protect the brand.

The easyGroup strategy is all about brand values. It lists several factors that are crucial to this aim and they are the sort of business lessons that could and should be applied to any small firm. They include offering great value, 'taking on the big boys', innovation, keeping it simple, being entrepreneurial and adopting a 'for the many not the few' attitude. Ultimately, the company's vision is, 'to develop Europe's leading value brand into a global force. We will paint the world orange!'

So that's the business. In terms of Stelios himself, he is realistic about his own abilities. 'I know most of my decisions are half chance anyway,' he says, 'so the sooner you realise that, the fewer mistakes you will make.'

He's too modest. Educated at the London School of Economics, he followed that with an MSc in Shipping, Trade and Finance from Cass Business School at City University, London. He worked for his father for a while in 1988 and, aged 25, set up his own shipping company, Stelmar shipping, a business he floated on the NYSE in 2001 and in 2005 it was sold to the OSG Shipping Group for approximately $1.3bn.

He was recognised by the Queen for entrepreneurship in 2006, receiving a knighthood. Queen Elizabeth apparently demonstrated her knowledge of budget airlines by telling the easyJet founder that she knew they were the UK's only direct service to Slovenia.

Stelios also supports a range of other charities and scholarships through his philanthropic foundation. So far, the flagship philanthropic programme has funded 10 scholarships each year at the London School of Economics and at City University's Cass Business School, 'fostering a new generation of innovative young European entrepreneurs with particular emphasis on students from the UK, Greece and Cyprus.'

In 2007 he created the 'Disabled Entrepreneur of the Year 'award in the UK in partnership with the Leonard Cheshire disability charity. The winner gets £50,000 towards his or her business.

Warming to the 'luck' theme, Stelios adds:

'Most people confuse luck with skill on the way up and blame everyone else including the weather, but not themselves, on the way down. The culture that allowed executives to place one-way bets with other people's money has a lot to do with this major correction in asset values. It inflated values in the first place.'

In terms of advice for businesses in difficult economic times, Stelios says cash is king. 'Only companies that conserve cash will survive and see the upturn. People with surplus cash will, in the next six to 18 months, be able to pick up assets at prices which will have corrected from the irrational exuberance level by a factor of 30%–70%.'

Stelios says there is no secret to his success. It's a question of hard work, simple branding, a cheap but solid service and, of course, 'some luck'.

Aaron Simpson

'Don't spend money if you can help it'

'If you believe in what you're doing and are confident you will bring people with you. My other piece of advice for the early days of running a business is: don't spend money if you can help it.' These are two reasons why Aaron Simpson's Quintessentially brand will, by the end of 2008, reach 70 countries and the business employ 1,500 people. It's been a phenomenal seven years for Simpson and co-founder Ben Elliot. Initially started as a London-based club, the 'lifestyle management' business now offers a wide range of global services to its rich and famous members, from wine to a chauffeur service, from a property search service to exclusive holiday destinations. Simpson says the aim is to become 'the Virgin of luxury'. And it's going the right way about it.

There are hundreds of concierge-type businesses catering for the needs of the rich and famous. Many clubs are localised, plus there are a plethora of corporate schemes dedicated to ensuring the needs of senior executives are taken care of. Where Quintessentially differentiates itself is in its top-end offering and global outlook.

Few competitors boast offices in Mozambique, Jeddah, Panama and Istanbul.

Simpson explains:

'In the beginning it took a lot of hard work and late nights convincing restaurants, clubs and other businesses to work with us. A lot of these places have their own lists of important clientele and didn't need us. But over time we convinced them and now if a well-known restaurant has a late cancellation for say 12 people, they come to us and ask us if we can help them fill it.'

Simpson says they realised early on that in any one city there are between 50 and 100 people you need to know. 'A lot of the top restaurants or clubs will be ultimately owned by a few people,' he says, 'so it was our mission to get to know all the important people.'

Having a celebrity heavy membership list also helped and a key part of the business plan was getting as many opinion formers as possible on board. 'We've had a lot of press because we looked after a lot of famous people,' Simpson says. 'From singers to footballers, high-flying business people to Royals, and the press are interested in that.' Socialite Jemima Khan says she's 'an ardent fan'; former model Sophie Dahl says the company is 'fantastic at organising all the things that you don't have the time (or the inclination) to do yourself' and Coldplay's PA calls Quintessentially 'indispensable'.

One reason, Simpson says, why the business has done well is because of the people it employs. He says it's about giving people a chance and giving them confidence to take decisions. 'We encourage people to have a go. If they get it wrong, then that's a lesson learned. If they make the same mistake twice that's another matter, that's not excusable.'

For many firms, expanding this quickly causes problems. Simpson sees it as a positive:

'By the end of 2010 we aim to be in 100 countries. That will make us pretty bulletproof in terms of problems in any one country, but then I think we already are. The people we deal with always have money to spend and although in certain countries the gap between rich and poor is growing, there are more and more people with money who want a company like ours to help them.'

Carlos Slim

'Reinvest profits'

Carlos Slim Helú is a Mexican telecoms entrepreneur and one of the richest men on the planet. Personally worth in the region of $35bn, he runs a large part of Mexico's telecoms industry and has influence throughout Latin America. He has been vice-president of the Mexican Stock Exchange, sits on the board of directors for Philip Morris International and he has built an important Mexican financial-industrial empire, Grupo Carso. In 1997, just before the company introduced its famous iMac line, Slim bought 3% of Apple Computer's stock, which turned out to be a very wise investment.

In reality, if you've ever been to Mexico, there's a fair chance you've been a client of his. From making phone calls to smoking cigarettes, he runs an empire of something like 200 companies in the country, including oil, commerce and tourism; you name it, he's probably involved.

Asked about the basis for the success of his business interests, Slim says the principles are 'simple structures, organisations with minimal hierarchies, personal development and internal training for executives.' He also cites the importance of quick decision-making and maintaining austerity in good times instead of expanding.

He says, 'Companies grow stronger if they are austere, capitalise revenues and accelerate development.'

It's been quite a life for Slim. His father emigrated to Mexico from Lebanon in 1902, aged just 14 and without a word of Spanish. Over time, through hard work and tenacity, he built up a business empire and was, in many ways, ahead of his time in terms of his attitude to business. Slim says,' By the 1920s he was already talking about an efficient business as one that sold large volumes at smaller margins, and with payment facilities, factors that today prevail in the large discount stores.'

Slim's father hammered home a strong business ethic in his children. He gave all five siblings a savings book with their usual weekly allowance, in order for them to learn to manage their income and expenses. They reviewed this book with him, analysing their expenses, purchases and activities, and by following this rule the children managed their finances. Aged just 12, Slim opened his first checking account and bought shares in Banco Nacional de México.

Slim says entrepreneurial creativity is key to the business of solving problems, and he has a very positive business outlook:

'Firm and patient optimism always yields its rewards. This is also one of my father's principles. All times are good times for those who know how to work and have the tools to do so; this is also from my father. What I learned is to always bear in mind that we leave with nothing, that we can only do things while alive and that we must be efficient, careful and responsible in managing our wealth to create more.'

He's certainly done that and there have been reports of Slim investing in Formula One, potentially in Team Honda. In 2008, he purchased a stake in The New York Times Company, making him the largest shareholder of those not related to the company's owners.

His Carso Global Telecom business holds the majority of the control shares of Telmex, which operates telecoms services in Mexico, as well as in Argentina, Brazil, Colombia, Chile, Ecuador, the US, Peru and Uruguay. The 1990 deal, in which Slim headed a group of investors that included France Télécom and Southwestern Bell Corporation in buying Telmex from the Mexican government, was questioned by some at the time, not least because the result was that the business now operates more than 90% of all telephone lines in Mexico. And the mobile phone company, Telcel, which Slim also controls, operates almost 80% of all the phones in the country. The deal enabled Slim to expand his telecoms interests throughout the region and over the past five years, his wireless carrier América Móvil has bought phone companies across Latin America, and is now the region's dominant company, with more than 100 million subscribers.

This success has led Slim to move away from telecoms into a wider range of business interests through his company Impulsora del Desarrollo y el Empleo en America Latina, or IDEAL. Its aim is to win major infrastructure projects throughout Mexico and Latin America. In addition, it is engaged in the construction and operation of water treatment plants, and is active in the health, and education sectors.

But with all that money, particularly in a poverty stricken country such as Mexico, Slim has followed the example of Bill Gates by stepping back from day-to-day business activity – his three sons now run the business empire while he remains chairman of IDEAL - and now Slim also invests in philanthropic projects.

His philanthropy began in 2000 when he helped organise the Mexico City Historic Downtown Foundation, whose objective is 'to revitalise and rescue Mexico City's historic downtown'. But he didn't stop there. Today, he heads the Latin America Development Fund project, which has a budget of more than $10bn to fund cultural projects throughout Latin America. Slim also gave $5.5m to the National Polytechnic Institute, one of the most important research universities in Latin America.

For Slim, the winner of countless awards for his business and increasingly philanthropic endeavours, it's a case of continually striving to improve. 'We were always active in modernisation, growth and training,' he says. 'We are confident that there is no challenge we cannot meet if we work together, with clear objectives and knowing the tools we have at our disposal. Money that leaves the company evaporates and that is why we reinvest profits.'

Guy Tullberg

'I don't let any retailer take more than 20%'

UK-based chutney, relish and sauce company Tracklements started trading in 1970. Founded by William Tullberg, the company began life selling his home-made mustard via local pubs and butchers. Today it employs 50 people, has a turnover of £4m, sells its wide range of products through more than 1,200 speciality delicatessens, butchers and farm shops across the UK, and is run by William's son, Guy. It produces up to 10,000 jars a day, using the original methods and recipes, and boasts a range of 50-plus different chutneys, pickles, relishes, jellies and mustards. And that's just the way Guy intends to keep it.

'Twenty years ago I don't think I really saw a big future in it,' Tullberg says. 'I just thought it kept dad busy. But over time the UK has become a lot more conscious of good food and we've capitalised on that. It makes me laugh when I see all these new, young food businesses talking up being all "innocent ". We've been innocent since 1970.'

Twelve years ago, the business decided to stop using a wholesale distributor to shift products to the nation's farm shops and butchers and to do the distribution itself. 'It set our sales back six months,' Tullberg says, 'meant we were processing 200 invoices a week instead of 10, meant we had to employ a lot more people to handle all the enquires and keep on top of it, but we haven't looked back.' Tullberg says that while wholesale distributors sell hundreds of different products, the change has meant that Tracklements now concentrates on itself.

'We're not looking to get Tracklements into the huge supermarkets,' Tullberg says. 'I actually think they are a graveyard for products. And also, I have a 20% rule. I don't let any retailer take more than 20% and the multiples would.'

Tullberg says his strict approach means the company retains the power and remains in control of its own destiny. But it does not indicate a lack of ambition. 'I'd say we're gently ambitious. But if anything, the market it moving towards us, rather than us chasing after the market, so I'm confident. And of course I'm confident in the products.'

Another innovation that Tullberg says makes a difference is using jars that stack:

'In the UK supermarkets, trays of sauces are put onto the shelves on trays so it's not important to be able to stack the jars. But in France they worked out if you remove the trays, they can fit more products on the shelves, so insist the glass jars stack. So we source

French jars that stack and supply the 1,200-plus specialist retailers that way, meaning they too can increase the number of products on their shelves.'

Tracklements claims to be the first company in the UK to introduce wholegrain mustard and to market onion marmalade, herb jellies and Cumberland sauce. As for the name of the business, Tullberg's great-grandmother used to sit at the end of the table on a typical Sunday lunch and ask other family members to 'pass the tracklements'.

Julie Meyer

'Raise money when you don't need it'

When the World Economic Forum calls you a 'Global Leader of Tomorrow' and you're voted one of the top 30 most powerful women in Europe by the *Wall Street Journal,* there is a sense that you may well have 'made it'. Plus it's the sort of praise that could go to one's head – but not Julie Meyer. The Sacramento, US-born chief executive of Ariadne Capital is far from aloof. On the contrary, she's understated and humble.

What are her greatest successes? 'My greatest achievements are emotional,' she says, 'not business related.' And those words are spoken by someone who founded, then sold, First Tuesday, a global network of entrepreneurs, for $50m in cash and shares. She has also, through Ariadne, a company she set up in August 2000, raised more than $100m of capital for start-ups, in addition to overseeing another $150m of seed capital found for start-ups through First Tuesday.

Although Meyer says her family 'can't figure out why I've spent all my adult life in Europe', it's been an incredibly successful time for her. Lauded for 'bringing the spirit of American venture capitalism to Europe', Meyer believes she has an unfair advantage: fearlessness. 'I'm restless and impatient and have a great sense that form is content. I can balance both, and that's how I package myself.' Meyer's European adventure began in Paris when she was 21. She says, 'I threw myself into Paris and went and figured it out. I had a sales job, working in French, and I realised people were buying into the whole package. I tried to play to my strengths, and one of those is communication.' Meyer took that realisation and came to England, where she went on to form the now legendary First Tuesday, a networking event which drew together all the movers, shakers, money men and wannabe internet start-ups to great effect.

It was the best and worst of times, says Meyer. Certainly, selling out at the peak of the internet bubble was good business, but the bubble soon burst. Yet Meyer remained committed to starting Ariadne Capital, a business formed for the express purpose of supporting new internet ventures. Wasn't that a bit of a risk? 'I feel that to work for someone is a risk,' says Meyer. 'I'd rather work for myself than join someone else's parade. I think that way you lessen the risk. I'm into building my own structures and because I'm building it, there's no glass ceiling.'

In terms of advice for others, Meyer says:

'Raise money when you don't need it. Also, capital is just a commodity and should be treated that way. It's just the fuel. People should bear in mind that there are many ways to get something funded. Also, don't do what you do because of the money. If you're good, the money will find you. The real asset is the entrepreneur's energy.'

Today, Meyer plans to set up a foundation and write a book aimed at girls in their teens to help them become addicted to achievement. She says:

'Men do what they do. Women wake up aged 45 and wonder what happened. The trouble with girls is that they don't get told they can do what they want. When they're young they are too busy worrying about getting and pleasing their boyfriends. I'm horrified the way girls' lives revolve around their boyfriends.'

If this effort is anything like the previous initiatives, look out girls; Julie Meyer is on a mission. 'This,' she says, 'is the age of the entrepreneur.'

NETWORKING

'If you don't know jewellery, know the jeweller'

Warren Buffett, chairman and CEO, Berkshire Hathaway

Mark Koska

'Research is vital'

Here's a good idea: a) come up with an invention that will save many millions of lives, then b) persuade governments around the world to pass legislation insisting their country's own health departments only stock the said life-saving invention. That's good business and that's exactly what Marc Koska, a UK-based inventor and entrepreneur, is doing.

Koska has devised a cheap but effective syringe that can only be used once. It took him 17 years to sell one. To date he's sold 700 million.

'In 1984 I read a newspaper article predicting the transmission of HIV through the re-use of needles and syringes,' he says. 'I was amazed and fascinated, and knew immediately that this was what I was going to do. Sadly, in 2006, this prediction has come horrifyingly true.' Koska was aged 23, working in various jobs, travelling around and living in the Caribbean, and sailing yachts. It was, he says, a seminal moment for him:

I had often heard statistics that the majority of new businesses and ideas fail within the first year or so. Why? Is it because they're all crap? No, they're in the wrong business or haven't done the right research. So for me to tackle this issue I had to not fall for the usual failure statistic. And for some strange reason, instead of instantly becoming an 'expert in syringes' I chose to learn all I could, as fast as possible, from the bottom up.'

He learnt about how drug addicts used syringes in the UK, went to Geneva to learn about public health policy, visited several syringe factories, studied plastic injection moulding, and read everything he could find on transmission of viruses such as HIV. 'I spent two years thinking about the problem,' he says. 'Then I started to come up with a solution.' His conclusion from this two-year learning curve was that syringe manufacturing held the key, so he set his sights on designing a syringe that manufacturers would want to make and sell.

His solution was the 'K1', and the reason it would work and he could sell it was that it could be made on existing tooling and assembly equipment with a small, very low-cost modification. This appealed to the manufacturers. Now, 15 countries around the world make the syringes, and each acts like a separate sales force for the company.

So far so good, but how did Koska persuade the world to buy it? The answer was simple. Koska started telling people about his invention: anybody and everybody who mattered in health. He gave talks. He approached government agencies and multinational aid organisations. As soon as one became interested and saw the very real benefits, the rest followed suit. But not only were governments impressed by the product, they realised that it was the only way forward. Countries such as Uganda, Indonesia and Bangladesh have since introduced legislation to ensure only Koska's syringes are used by their health departments.

The reality of the situation was brought home to him during a trip to India. On the streets, Koska saw small, bare-footed children out collecting used syringes to resell them for money. His syringes, which cannot be used twice, will eradicate this sort of practice, not to say help the many millions of people around the world avoid sharing needles for injections.

Turnover for Koska's company, Star Syringe, has reached $1.5m, a figure that has tripled in the last three years and is set to continue in that vein from now on. The company was awarded the Queen's Award for Enterprise in 2006 as a direct result of this.

Finally, a former Inventor of the Year, Koska's contribution to global healthcare has resulted in his being presented with an OBE by the Queen for International Trade this year. It's recognition of two decades of life-saving work and enterprise, and is a lesson for any would-be inventor.

Riky Ash

'Be multi-talented'

What have British comedian Ronnie Corbett, actress Hermione Norris and half the cast of popular British TV show *Last of the Summer Wine* got in common? Well, for one, they have all been stunt-doubled by Riky Ash. His business, called Falling For You, has been running for 14 years and in that time Ash has accumulated more than 350 television and film credits. He's even featured in the *Guinness Book of Records* by holding the record for the world's most versatile stuntman. He's doubled for actors ranging from 3 ft 6 in to 6 ft 4 in tall (Ash himself is 5 ft 3 in), and for people aged six to 87.

But his work is not all about leaping out of burning buildings and having bottles smashed over his head. Early in his career, Ash realised that the more strings he had to his bow the better. So, in addition to being a Fifth Dan Shaolin Kung-Fu expert, he can handle horses, cars, motorbikes, stunts based around fire, swimming, and powerboats; he does heights; he ice skates and will happily fall down staircases. If that wasn't enough, he's also a trained actor, something Ash soon realised would make him that much more appealing to production crews.

'If a TV company are shooting a scene where someone crashes through a window, then gets up and runs off, it's better for them not to have to cut from the stunt to the actor and worry about continuity issues,' he says. That means he's gained a range of acting/ stunt work that would have gone to two people in the past.

As a youth, Ash says he was never a daredevil. If anything, he was the complete opposite. But getting in to martial arts opened his eyes. He represented Great Britain at the German Open (taking first place in 'Kung-Fu destruction') and, talking to the other competitors, started to find out more about how he could make serious money doing stunts or fight work on television. 'I enlisted in drama school and contacted the UK actors union Equity. Then, I started going out and observing other stuntmen at work, helping out and learning from what they were doing. I hired stunt videos and got books out of the library.' Basically, he did his research.

He hasn't looked back. Since joining Equity he's constantly worked. 'There are a lot of average stuntmen,' Ash says. 'But because I have many skills and can act I'm in demand.' Before he started the stunt work, Ash earned £6,000 a year as a cabinet maker. He can now earn that in under a week. Getting doused in petrol and set on fire can earn him £3,000, as can throwing himself off a cliff. This is scary work, even for Ash, who openly admits he can be frightened doing certain stunts, but a pretty good rate for work that last a matter of seconds. 'The best payer is television,'he says, 'particularly a show like *Last of the Summer Wine*, because you get an 80% repeat fee and you get paid if it runs overseas, too. I've done about 50 episodes.'

Falling For You's turnover is around £150,000 (although some years he can earn up to £250,000). That's not bad for a sole trader, especially when all his outlay comes to about £15,000 annually. 'I'm not complacent, though,' Ash says. 'I still contact all the production companies and produce marketing material about me and the business.' Ash says he's considered going to the US to work but he's got enough to occupy him here for the time being.

'I've been a success because I'm versatile, reliable and honest. I'm not a big fan of business books. To me, it's all about common sense.'

Stefan Wissenbach

'What's your unique ability?'

Stefan Wissenback believes it is important for entrepreneurs to know what their unique ability is, although many people don't make the best use of that ability because of poor time management.

Stefan Wissenbach is chairman of the Wissenbach Group, a wealth management and investment consultancy that works with high net worth clients. The company employs 22 people and its clients are worth anything from £3m to £100m. For Wissenbach, personal development is the secret of his success.

Every 90 days he flies to Chicago where, along with a small number of American entrepreneurs, he sees an entrepreneurial coach. 'To get on this course you need to be able to prove your personal worth is more than half a million pounds,' Wissenbach says. 'One guy on it is the second largest land owner in Brazil. So these are serious and wealthy business people and they want to learn more. I think a lot of entrepreneurs in the UK think they know it all already.'

Mentoring has taught Wissenbach many things, but the most important revolve around time management. He explains:

'First of all, what is your unique ability? Most entrepreneurs will be working on so many things that they are not making the most of that ability. That's why it is important to split up your days into free days, focus days and buffer days. The free days are when you have no interaction with work. If you're fresh you think better. Focus days are days you spend 80% of your time on what you do best. Buffer days are for planning.'

Wissenbach sets himself goals: three-year, one-year, 90-day and one-month goals that he writes down and sticks to. 'It helps you build a picture and remain focussed,' he says. 'And it gives you something to work towards.' But it's not just business. He sets himself family goals and fitness goals. 'A lot of entrepreneurs work six days a week and have a string of broken relationships and marriages behind them, but it doesn't have to be like that.'

Wissenbach used to work six days a week and take two weeks' holiday. Then he saw a business coach who advised him to work four days a week and take eight weeks' holiday a year. What was the result? 'We doubled our profits in the following year.'

But it's not all about profit. Wissenbach works hard to motivate his staff by handing out a weekly award for effort and doing quarterly away-days. Last month the whole company learned how to make cocktails. 'All our staff get a personal development plan that is reviewed every 90 days,' Wissenbach says. 'It doesn't take up a lot of time and it's an investment in people that we are happy to make. The more time and effort we invest in people, the harder and better they work.'

'A lot of entrepreneurs are always chasing the pot of gold at the end of the rainbow but when they get to the end they're often disappointed. For me, it's important to enjoy the journey.'

Paul Titley

'I always try to hire people I know and trust'

UK-based R5 Pharmaceuticals makes medicines. A biotech company will approach it with a quantity of powdered drug, and R5 turns it into small batches of pills that are then used for clinical testing. The company helps the biotechs consider the best size, shapes, textures and taste of the pills, and has the expertise to control at what point in the body the pill dissolves and releases the drugs. It's super-specialist, high-tech stuff. And within the first two years of trading the firm already employs 30 staff and is turning over £2m.

The founder and CEO of the business, Paul Titley, worked at medical research organisation Wellcome for 25 years until it was taken over by Glaxo when 'the writing was on the wall' in terms of Titley's job. He then worked for another biotech firm, Quintiles, before moving to Scotland-based drug delivery firm Encap. Then he decided to go it alone, working as a consultant, and was asked by BioCity in Nottingham, to write up a business plan for a large building, which had been formerly owned by Knoll and abandoned full of high-tech drug-related lab equipment. The more Titley thought about it, the more he thought he could start a business that utilised the space and equipment. So he called up former colleagues and asked them to join him.

'We had this great building but no revenue, not many staff and no actual work to do,' Titley says. 'Somehow, and I'm still not sure how, R5 managed to acquire a small chemistry group that had revenues but no laboratory. A meeting of two desperate people, you might say. And we were on our way.'

A major breakthrough for R5 was signing a contract with Japanese giant Mitsubishi. Although perhaps best known for cars, the company has a bewildering range of business interests, and one of them is pharmaceuticals. Paul says,

'The chief science officer at R5, David Jordan, has spent a lot of time in his career going to Japan, and he had a great network of people who know and respect him. The relationships bore fruit when a Mitsubishi representative came across R5 at a trade show. Back in Japan he asked around about R5 and because of David, we got a lot of glowing references. On the strength of that, and after a delegation came to the UK, we signed a contract.'

The contract means Mitsubishi recommends R5 to Japanese clients, plus it gives the business fantastic kudos.

Titley also puts the success of the business to date on the number of high quality people the company has attracted. 'I always try to hire people I know and trust,' he says. 'It means you can quickly get to the point where you can disagree without tip-toeing around and worrying about upsetting someone's feelings.'

Titley says the over-50 are often the first to go when the large pharmaceutical companies merge, but that's great news for him and R5 because they can snap up the talent. Titley relies on continuous networking and subscribing to databases offering pharmaceutical-focussed intelligence to keep on top of the latest happenings in the industry. And so far, the results are good. The company is on track to expand to 50 employees and move into new inhalation-related drug products.

Debbie Leary

'Networking and innovation'

Debbie Leary's policeman husband was off to Toronto, Canada, for a conference about the latest forensic techniques. She was about to start a new career as an English literature lecturer, had three weeks off and decided to join him in Canada to check out the city. But, by her own admission, Leary is nosy and she attended the conference as well. It was here, or rather in the bar afterwards, that she had a eureka moment. She explains:

'The English police men were talking about using things called 'stepping plates' while at a forensic crime scene. These enable them to stay off the floor while carrying out their investigations. The Canadians had never heard of them, so I wrote a couple of notes about that on some hotel notepaper.'

That event took place in 2001. Since then Leary has given up the teaching, started her business, called Forensic Pathways, raised £60,000 from the bank, sourced tooling from China, won entrepreneur and innovation awards, and now employs 10 people. The company has gone from stepping plates (now being featured on US TV cop show *CSI Miami* & *CSI New York* to supplying a range of more than 1,300 forensic products, with distributors in Australia, China, the US, the Netherlands and Turkey.

The company also runs a training/consultancy service for a range of organisations about forensic issues, working with some 50 associate experts in the field. Plus, thanks to in-house research and development, the business has moved into the knowledge management arena with the provision of an analytical software tool 'Maverick', which assists companies and public services in the identification of fraud, criminal networks, and identity theft. Microsoft is so impressed they have made them a 'Case Study' and they are being nominated for 'Lighthouse Status' as world leaders in the provision of 'software as a service'.

But (back to the police story) on returning to the UK after the 2001 conference, Leary decided to call up various police forces around the country and ask them what they needed in terms of forensic equipment. She was stunned:

'No one had ever asked them what they wanted. They were simply told what there was. So when I began asking them how they would improve various equipment and what would make their lives easier, they gladly told me. I've got no great knowledge of the forensic arena, but I spotted that people had problems and we tried and still try, to address them.

'I think if I had two secrets of success for this business,' Leary adds, 'it is networking and innovating.' What was plainly obvious to Leary when she first saw a stepping plate was that 1) it was made from aluminium and 2) they couldn't be stacked neatly. 'I imagine at a crime scene it's important to be able to see the floor,' Leary says, 'but no one had thought of making these plates from a see-through material. So that's what we did and, of course, everyone agreed it was a good idea.'

In terms of networking, Leary is well-placed. She was appointed to the board of the UK Government-backed Small Business Council in November 2006 and as a supplier to the UN sits on the UK UN Global Compact Network. Both give her access to big networks of people, plus it gives her business massive credibility.

'I was watching the news about the Iraq war and saw that the Iraqi forces were being trained by non-qualified people. I thought about how we might be able to help, in terms of the specialist forensics knowledge we have at our disposal, and that's how the UN thing came about.'

In part, Forensic Pathways' success has resulted from the increasingly dangerous world we live in. With global terrorism seemingly on the rise, the need for experts in forensics is also on the up.

But isn't this a long way from teaching Chaucer? 'In many ways, what I'm doing now is also about telling stories,' Leary says. 'Today, we help people piece together stories, either through forensic research, equipment or techniques, or through using our computer software to gain real knowledge from the information company's hold.'

Carole Stone

'I spend time nurturing friendships'

Some people are well-connected. Others know someone who knows someone else. And then there is Carole Stone. She has a database of almost 30,000 contacts, throws regular networking salons, mixing up people from a bewildering range of industries and businesses, and holds an annual Christmas party attended by anything up to 2,000 friends. On paper, it's easy to be cynical about Carole Stone and her networking lifestyle-cum-business. How can one person really have 30,000 contacts and really know 2,000 people to invite to a Christmas party? But in Stone's case it's true. They all know her. More than that, they like her and sing her praises.

In person, it's easy to understand how she has carved out such a unique position. 'I like people,' she says, 'and I assume people will like me. I'm interested in people and I'm unthreatening.' Of course there is more to it than that. For all her calm exterior, Stone is the first to admit that having so many contacts is actually very hard work.

'I spend time nurturing friendships,' she says. 'I make notes about everyone, about events and details in their lives. And then, when I come home at the end of an evening or after a lunch, I debrief myself and write everyone down on my computer.' So the next time she sees them she can ask about the kids, the holiday, the appointment with the doctor.

Stone's remarkable contact list dates from her time working as producer on BBC Radio 4's *Any Questions* in the 1970s. All manner of politicians, business leaders, media types and luminaries from any number of industries passed through. And Stone kept in contact with them. It also gave her a real insight into people; for however famous or media-friendly they might appear, all suffered from nerves or tension when put in front of a microphone; they all needed help in one way or another.

And what started as an excuse for Stone to introduce her mother to all these wonderful people resulted in a full-time occupation:

'I started doing drinks parties and everyone I invited came along. Then, the CEO of a big company asked me if I could arrange for the movers and shakers in a particular industry to get together in an informal setting so his senior managers could find out all the current thinking. He wanted to do eight sessions and I agreed to do it. I thought I was doing it for £800, but I'd misheard him and a cheque came through for £8,000.'

Stone says her philosophy is 'seize the moment'. 'People should try things and see what happens. Do what you want to do. I always wanted to be a TV star but it never happened. But I tried and I'm satisfied I gave it my best shot.'

In terms of networking, her advice is simple, 'Be generous with your contacts and keep in touch with your rivals. I always invite mine to my parties. And always ask everyone how they are or how they feel. People love that. Also, give yourself a time limit to spend at a party and stick to it.'

LEADERSHIP

'To succeed in life, you need two things: ignorance and confidence'

Mark Twain, US author

Sergey Brin

'Keep it simple'

Sergey Brin is co-founder and 'president of technology' at online search engine Google, a business he founded in 1998 with fellow Stanford University student Larry Page. Like Hoover, Google has become a verb, which tells you everything you need to know about how widespread and well-known the simple-looking search engine has become. The company's mission is to organise the world's information and make it universally accessible and useful. Incidentally, 'Googol' is the mathematical term for a 1 followed by 100 zeros and Google's play on the term reflects the company's mission to organise the immense amount of information available on the web.

The company now employs 20,000 people worldwide and its market capitalisation, on NASDAQ, is around $113bn. Brin is said to be worth an estimated $18.5bn, making him the 26 richest person in the world and the fifth richest person in the United States. Aged 35, he is the fourth-youngest billionaire in the world.

It goes without saying that one of his main interests at university was search engine technology. He has published more than a dozen academic papers on the topic, including 'Extracting Patterns and Relations from the World Wide Web'; 'Dynamic Data Mining: A New Architecture for Data with High Dimensionality' and the seminal paper 'The Anatomy of a Large-Scale Hypertextual Web Search Engine'.

And despite the complicated-sounding nature of these papers, for Brin, simplicity is the key. 'A lot of the early search engines took indexing for granted,' he says. 'It was a fairly simple idea – you take all the information and create an index. And then we developed a way of ranking the websites. It seems obvious now but before we started Google, ranking websites wasn't considered important.' Brin credits Google co-founder Larry Page as being the one who pursued the idea that collecting the information was important. 'We came up with notion that not all web pages are created equal, unlike people,' Brin says. 'Some are less important than others.'

Google patented its PageRank technology, which basically interprets a link from page A to page B as a vote, by page A, for page B. But Google looks at more than the sheer volume of votes, or links a page receives; it also analyses the page that casts the vote. Votes cast by pages that are themselves 'important' weigh more heavily and help to make other pages 'important'. Brin says that in the early days, they simply tried to create a better search engine than already existed. 'We thought we'd give it a try,' he says. 'There was no real downside to trying and we only needed a little bit of funding.'

As with its technology, Google has chosen to ignore conventional wisdom in designing its business. The company started with seed money from angel investors and brought together two competing venture capital firms to fund its first equity round. While the dotcom boom exploded around it and competitors spent millions on marketing campaigns to 'build brand', Google focussed instead on quietly building a better search engine.

Google's managers then identified two initial opportunities for generating revenue: search services and advertising. Today, the business makes its money from products such as AdWords and AdSense. Google AdWords advertisers create ads to drive qualified traffic to their sites and generate leads. Google publishing partners deliver those ads targeted to relevant search results powered by Google AdSense. With AdSense, the publisher shares in the revenue generated when readers click the ads.

Early on in the company's history, the two founders worked on making the search engine technology scalable. Today, Google receives daily search requests from all over the world, including Antarctica. Users can restrict their searches for content in 35 non-English languages, including Chinese, Greek, Icelandic, Hebrew, Hungarian and Estonian. 'I'd say 80% of the work we do is the same across all countries,' Brin says. 'It's the reason we've been successful. Unlike some of our competitors, it's simple and scalable.'

Brin says the Chinese and Korean markets have proved to be slightly more challenging, in terms of connectivity issues and in terms of language differences, but even then, 70% of what Google does in China is the same as the US.

'There are complicated government relationship issues in China, and trade issues and policy questions. We can't predict what will happen, but we try to stay in touch with people we know who are in touch with China and who know it. Ultimately, we deduced that our participation in that market is positive, for us and for the people of China.'

Brin says thoughts about his competitors don't keep him up at night. He says:

'It's important those types of things don't keep you up. You might have heard of some of our competitors, micro... soft is it? I know a lot of people in a big company like Google do worry, but what is more valuable is to spend time thinking about the incredible opportunity we have. We have a lot of resources and great people. We have an opportunity to create new things.'

According to Google co-founder Larry Page, 'The perfect search engine would understand exactly what you mean and give back exactly what you want.' Given the state of search technology today, that's a far-reaching vision requiring research, development and innovation; and that's where Google comes in. Its ultimate aim is to provide a much higher level of service to all those who seek information, whether they're at a desk in Boston, driving through Bonn or strolling in Bangkok.

Google says it has worked out several things in business that it has found to be true. It's best to do one thing really, really well, that fast is better than slow, that you can be serious without wearing a suit – and that great just isn't good enough.

Finally, Brin says the reason the technology and business have been a success is because of his fundamental passion for computer science. 'It's important to do what you love,' he says. 'And I really love computer science and math in general.'

Sergey Brin was addressing the University of California, Berkeley.

Steve Leach

'A strong infrastructure is important from the start'

'We practise what we preach.' That, says Steve Leach, founder of search engine marketing firm Bigmouthmedia, is the secret of his success – and what success. He founded the Edinburgh-based business in 1996 and it evolved into one with more than 250 blue-chip clients and a £14m turnover. In late 2006, the firm merged with German equivalent GlobalMedia in a deal backed by The Carlyle Group. As of mid-2007, the Munich-based Global Media CEO Thomas Gerteis stepped down, leaving Leach in control. Clients include Hilton, British Airways and AOL, and the business has doubled its number of employees in offices that now reach from Edinburgh to Milan, from Moscow to Seoul.

Leach says:

'I was working as a firefighter in the early 1990s, and in that job when it's tough, it's really tough, but when it's quiet, you have a lot of time on your hands to study or think. The internet was just starting and I was fascinated by it. I suppose I always wanted to strike out on my own and this looked like it could provide the opportunity.'

Leach and his wife considered a number of internet-related business ideas but kept coming back to marketing and the potential of online marketing and advertising, something the pair were interested in.

'There was no Google, I think it was AltaVista and one other, so we advertised ourselves online, explaining to people that if they wanted help with their online marketing and ads, then come to us. We worked hard on the algorithms and other technical stuff and we ensured we came up top of the searches. What we realised was that people in a variety of industries and business also wanted to come out top of searches and the business went from there.'

Early on in the company's history, Leach ensured there was a split between home and work. He borrowed money from his father and invested in premises. 'Keeping costs down at the beginning was vital,' Leach says. 'But property is a good investment anyway, so we bought an office and I made sure I kept work and home life separate - even if it meant me working at the office until 2am, grabbing four hours sleep at home and then going back to the office.' The early investment paid off.

Recalling Bigmouthmedia's big break he says:

'We got a meeting with clickmusic in London. They were something to do with Virgin at the time and I remember that being our big break. How did we get the meeting? Well, they looked for search engine marketing online and we came out top. It's how we got that bit of business and by far the way we get most of our business. It amazes me that companies who set themselves up as search engine marketing firms aren't anywhere near the top of the searches themselves.'

After that, Leach says it's doing what they say they will, offering a great service and being competitively priced which makes them a success. (knowing something most other people on the planet don't – how to get to the top of search engines, also has something to do with it). He explains:

'People think there is something of the black arts when it comes to internet-related stuff. And there are a lot of firms out there who will take the money and not provide the service. But I'm a big believer in what goes around comes around. What I've seen in this industry is that people move around a lot. I come across senior people in the digital industries who have worked at five or six major corporations. And when they move jobs, they come back to us. We're good and we're straight with people.'

Merging with the German business was prefaced by many sleepless nights, but Leach reckons the companies fit together well and he's as excited as ever about the potential for growth. 'The merger taught me the value of good advice, from people who have been there and done it. It also taught me the importance of a strong infrastructure from the outset, that isn't reliant on one person at the top.'

But for now, Leach is the person at the top.

Eddie Czestochowski

'You get nothing for nothing'

Hard work is key for Czestochowski. 'Everyone called me Eddie,' explains the managing director of Cell Pack Solutions, Eddie Czestochowski. 'Because no one can pronounce my surname, everyone remembers me. It's really helped me over the years.' There's a bit more to Eddie's success than his name. Firstly, the fact that his business is so niche. His company sells batteries: any type, all types. The batteries you're told no longer exist – Eddie can find them. The battery for that old electric toothbrush or for that brand new diving computer – Eddie's business can get them. The business has been so successful that from setting up as a sole trader in 1998, he now employs 12 full-time staff. 'My first order was worth £6 and was to refurbish a battery pack for a calculator,' he says. 'The chap had been told to throw it away but he didn't want to. Then he found me.' In his first month, Eddie's turnover was £300; by the end of the first year it was £80,000 and he is now on target to hit that figure as a monthly average.

Eddie used to be a salesman for a battery company and thought a) he could do it better and b) he could do without driving across the country all week. He gave up a well-paid job and, he says, most people thought he was mad.

An early turning point for Eddie was his entering a British Telecom-backed competition to write 50 words about what a new website would mean to your company. Eddie was shortlisted and interviewed by a man from BT who not only liked the idea of the business, but he also had a problem finding a particular battery. Eddie came joint-second, won £4,000, a laptop computer and £1,500 towards the setting up of a website.

'After a year or so I was getting so many enquiries I was finding it hard to cope,' Eddie says. 'The problem was that I was the only person who could deal with the queries. So I decided to download my skills and knowledge onto a spreadsheet so that anyone could pick up the phone and deal with questions about batteries.' It was a bright move. The database now lists thousands of battery types, complete with pictures and information about them, enabling Eddie to grow the business the way he has.

It also resulted in Cell Pack winning a number of technology innovation awards, both locally and nationally, something Eddie swears by:

'Some people view awards as an ego trip, but you cannot win if you do not enter. You should use the entry forms as an opportunity to review your business and to benchmark your activities. Plus it's a great opportunity to gain free PR and enhance your profile - it makes absolute sense.'

Eddie's parents came to the UK as Polish immigrants after the Second World War and their hardworking attitude is something he feels is ingrained in him:

'They had nothing, worked hard and that was the way I was brought up. You get nothing for nothing. I suppose I work too hard but I love it. Some people think it's strange knowing so much about batteries, but I don't care. People come to me and say they can't find a particular battery and I see that as a challenge – especially if they've been told that they won't be able to find another like it. I like helping people; it's as simple as that.'

Ian Millner

'If you don't take risks, you won't get anywhere'

'I had my annual review today,' says Ian Millner, founder of London-based creative agency iris. 'I've done all right this year. I got good marks in terms of passion, clarity of vision, working hard and having exacting standards. Perhaps one area I need to work on, though, is getting people to tell me what they really think instead of what they think I want to hear.' It's a familiar scenario, and perhaps unavoidable when, like Millner, you've grown a business from nothing to a business with more than 250 employees in offices stretching from London to New York, from Manchester to Singapore.

'I see myself as the pace setter,' Millner adds. 'Although I think celebrating progress is important, I don't really enjoy what we've done. I'm always thinking about what's ahead. In that respect, some staff may find me intimidating.' It's another thing to work on post-annual review.

The business has grown into one worth £50m since its inception in 1999. As is typical in many industries, Millner felt he could do it better so decided to leave the agency he was at and go it alone. Well, with a few other like-minded individuals as well. 'When I look back the risks were quite small,' he says. 'They seemed big at the time but in retrospect I wish we'd taken more risk. And I especially wish we'd raised all the money ourselves.'

Millner's business is all about helping other companies in terms of their marketing and positioning. It's about building brands and using various media to do so. Today, its client list includes organisations as diverse as Manchester United FC, Lego and Amnesty International. In the beginning, the list wasn't quite so long. In fact, it consisted of one client, albeit a good one: Ericsson.

'From the outset we decided to focus on telecoms and marketing to youth,' says Millner. 'And we were very good at it. Over time we picked up other, small clients, then a big break came with us being appointed to work on a UK government sexual health campaign.' Millner's exacting standards were one of the reasons behind getting these sorts of clients. He explains:

'The pitching process was very formal and very hard work. One of the deciding factors in us winning those big pitches was, and is, our heavy use of our own research. We've done it from day one and it underpins what we're about. It enables us to tell the client something they don't know, even at the stage of the pitch. And that's impressive.'

In terms of managing the organisation, Millner isn't alone. In fact he turns to a former boss who acts as a mentor, not just for him but for all the senior managers in the company. 'Sometimes people lack that little bit of confidence to do what they think is right. There's a self-imposed barrier. This guy comes in and encourages them to think for themselves and do what they think it right.' Millner admits he's made mistakes over the years but stresses the importance of taking risks. 'For a business to be a success it's important to make mistakes and learn from them,' he says. 'If you don't take risks, you won't get anywhere.'

Jay Bregman

'Use university research'

American Jay Bregman, chief technical officer at London-based eCourier, was studying entrepreneurship at the London School of Economics when he started working on an idea. He did a thesis on electronic document exchange and, for a case study, looked into motorcycle courier companies in London. He spoke to a range of businesses working in this area, interviewing them about how they operated. He expected to find all the major firms using state-of-the-art IT systems. The reality was very different.

He found very little perception of a need for change in the industry and says:

'A lot of courier companies have been in the industry for 20 years and don't see why they should change. They think what we're doing is a fad and that it will pass. And anyway, to offer what we do, they would need to spend a lot of money and most simply don't have it.'

The strength of what Bregman's company offers is in its technology. Two years in the making, the system could transform the industry. With it, 90% of bookings are made online. Customers input the collection address and delivery addresses, then choose the vehicle type. The process is quick and simple. The computer then works out who the optimum courier is for the delivery, taking into account information it has learned from previous jobs as well as traffic and weather conditions. That courier is then instructed electronically to proceed to your pick-up location. All of this is done via GPS which also tracks riders' positions every 10 seconds, enabling customers to do the same.

On the one hand it's smart. On the other, it's good for the couriers. Put simply, riding anything around London is dangerous. Working as a courier is one of the most dangerous jobs there is, so it's not the type of work one enters into as a career. You get in, earn as much as possible, try to stay alive, and get out. Through eCourier's technology, the cyclists and motorcyclists can do up to 50% more jobs per day.

Bregman's studies enabled him to do a lot of the business planning and research before taking the plunge. He says:

'By the time of the investment round, we had plans, had developed as far as possible the technological outline of what we wanted to do, found suppliers and had contracts in place and we were ready to go. So in the morning, I was going around asking for half a million pounds of funding; in the afternoon I was going to lectures.'

The dual approach paid off. After initially raising £100,000, the summer of 2004 saw another £700,000 raised and the business was ready to go.

When it came to overcoming the logistical problems involved with tracking riders via GPS, Bregman turned to academic institutions. 'I asked myself who was writing or researching short haul logistics,' he says. 'I soon found there were 10 universities around the world, such as Stanford and MIT, who had departments looking into aspects of this, so I approached them with my problem.'

It paid off. By year-end the business forecasts it will be doing 40,000 deliveries a month with around 135 couriers. Turnover is already more than £4m in an industry estimated to be worth from £300m to £400m.

'For me, the role models were eBay, Amazon, Yahoo! and later Google,' Bregman says. 'These entrepreneurial businesses proved that, in a small way, you can change the world. I think with all of them, and us, the approach is on customer service. I think it's ingrained in Americans that the customer is always right. It's a great asset for us to have.'

Theo Paphitis

'Stay ahead of the game'

The owner of stationers Ryman, Theo Paphitis believes that it's important to look ahead in business and set targets. He offers entrepreneurs the following advice:

'My advice to entrepreneurs and start-ups is don't think this recession is anything like the one in the 1980s and 1990s because it's not. This is much worse. The UK Government is making it up as it goes along; the Bank of England is making it up, as is the Fed in the States. There's no precedent. My advice to all people running businesses is "be afraid, be very afraid." But also, they should be excited. I think people should be experiencing those two emotions and that will help them take their business forward. But don't imagine it's going to be easy. It's going to be a rollercoaster ride, that's for sure.'

Born in Limassol, Cyprus, in 1959, Paphitis and his family emigrated to England when he was six-years-old. Paphitis started his career at the age of 16 as a tea boy/filing clerk with Lloyds of London insurance brokers before making his first foray into retail at the age of 18. At the age of 20 he moved into finance, specialising in turnarounds. He set up his own company at the age of 23.

He decided at an early age that he had to work for himself:

'I used to get frustrated when I was younger. I was dyslexic; I had this funny accent and didn't go to a posh university or get any decent exam results. I used to think I was stupid. But I realised that it wasn't me who was stupid, it was other people. I had common sense but those around me didn't. I was spotting opportunities that no one else was but working for others held me back. So I decided I had to work for myself or end up having a frustrating life.'

In the following years he purchased, and turned around, ailing companies such as sports advertising firm Movie Media Sports, Ryman the stationer, the Contessa and La Senza lingerie chains, and Partners, another stationer. His method, he admits, is simple. The most important aspect of any of his takeover deals is spotting the right business to buy and pulling out if the deal wasn't right.

In talking about the importance of confidence in business, he says:

'Confidence is important in business but don't confuse that with arrogance. I'm not arrogant enough to think I know it all because I don't. I spent a long time working on a deal recently but walked away from it after spending a lot of money on it. I was confident enough to spend the time and money on it but I knew when to pull out and admit that it didn't make sense. My skill in business over the years has been working out what deals to do and what deals to turn down.'

And this, Paphitis says, is down to doing his homework:

'Not only did I have the answers for any questions I might be asked, but if something was an issue, I made sure it was highlighted and I had the solution to it as well. If you've got the what-ifs buttoned down (because they will occur, as sure as eggs is eggs) you'll be able to convince people to support you.'

Doing that has been one of Paphitis's biggest strengths over the years. His experience and knowledge of the money markets has helped him in terms of where and how to raise funds for a takeover, but his persuasive abilities, and his charm, have also helped. But he hasn't done it alone and often talks about 'we' when it comes to his business success. 'I couldn't have done what I've done without a lot of people around me,' he says. 'There are maybe three or four people around me who I'm closest to, but they have people around them and ultimately, it's everyone in the businesses I operate who are important to the success. I know that I have a limited ability myself.'

He's too modest. All the firms he has bought into have been turned around and made profitable by stripping out the unprofitable parts, upgrading IT networks to make purchasing simpler and getting the product offerings right.

'When it comes to growing a business, rule number one is there must be a market,' he says. 'Without a market, there's no business. It's very difficult and expensive to create a market for a product or service. I've never created a market in my life. But I've put my money where my mouth is. If there is a market, rule number two is cash. Without cash, it's doomed.'

The market for lingerie was certainly there when Paphitis was asked if he was interested in La Senza, but by his own admission, he didn't have a clue about underwear. It was the only high street boutique chain providing 'sexy, comfortable and romantic lingerie and nightwear at affordable prices'. But Paphitis and his team quickly realised that with better stock control, being more generous with the sizing and small touches such as a free gift-wrapping service, it could make all the difference.

La Senza was sold in July 2006 to Lion Capital, a private equity company, but Paphitis remains on the board and retains a minority shareholding. Contessa was also sold. So today, Paphitis concentrates on the stationery business. Although he's expecting a difficult year in 2009, he's not downbeat.

'For me, it's probably the most exciting period in my business life,' he says. 'I'm like a puppy in the mornings, and I can't wait to put the TV on and see the latest news. There are deals to be done!' Paphitis says being excited about business is what it's all about. 'If you're not excited by it, if you can't bore your mates down the pub with it, don't do it.'

But don't forget to listen to advice. 'You must be able to listen – and not have selective hearing. Ask difficult questions and take the criticism on board.' Listening to business ideas has become a new occupation for Paphitis thanks to his inclusion as one of the 'Dragons' on TV's *Dragons' Den*, where he witnesses all manner of hare-brained schemes.

Ultimately, he says all businesses must constantly move forward. He adds:

'A business that stands still is a business that goes backwards. You've got to be constantly looking at being ahead of the game, putting in new initiatives, and keeping everybody busy. Set new targets each year and your staff will get more experience – and the business will stay fresh and move faster.'

Jill Barker

'Celebrity endorsement'

Canadian Jill Barker worked in derivatives in the City of London for 10 years. Then she got pregnant, and then she was made redundant. As a result of her son's nappy rash and a fruitless search for environmentally friendly nappies, Barker decided there might be a market for such products so in the autumn of 1999, she opened a shop in north London and called it Green Baby.

'I had idyllic visions of sitting in the shop, with baby, selling nappies and other products and having a lovely time,' she says. 'I think that lasted about three days.'

But while sitting in a shop all day didn't live up to Barker's expectations, she found herself on the crest of a green wave. 'People were coming from miles around to buy the nappies so I started doing mail order,' she says. 'A year later we got a website up and running and the business now stocks hundreds of different product ranges.'

Barker says the name 'Green Baby' is one of the single most important reasons why the business has gone on to do well. 'I found the name and found that no one else was using it, so registered it quick. Today there are many different companies selling baby related and 'green' products via their websites, but I think we've got the best name.'

It also runs four shops in London and sells 40% of its goods to customers in the US. One reason for the popularity stateside is that Barker is something of a green celebrity. 'Julia Roberts bought some of our nappies, recommended by her friend Gwyneth Paltrow. They have both spoken about the nappies and that's the sort of publicity you can't buy.' Halle Berry is another customer and it all means increased interest and sales for Barker.

'In retrospect,' she says, 'I do wish I'd taken more of a risk and borrowed money to grow quicker, but then saying that my turnover is £3m and it's all mine.' Barker is also savvy when it comes to selling own-brand goods through the site, rather than just selling other people's stuff. 'It takes more time, of course, and costs more to do it, but I think it's important. A lot of online businesses in this market sell our products. So my competitors, people who have copied what we're doing, sell our products, which is good business.'

One of Barker's biggest challenges is living up to the green tag. When major UK supermarket Tesco sold Green Baby products, Barker received hate mail. 'Some of it was vicious, but it doesn't make sense to attack us. We're trying to get more and more people going green, and if by stocking Green Baby products in Tesco helps do that, what's the problem?'

Barker says the green movement is here to stay and she feels she's at the beginning of something rather than the end, although she sees herself moving into new directions in the coming years: organic dog food, for one. 'Do you know how much people spend on their pets each year...?'

Michael Jackson

'Without the right quality of people you will never grow a successful business'

Michael Jackson knows from experience how important it is to employ quality people in order to grow a business and that such people need to be paid the market rate.

In recalling his start as an entrepreneur, he says:

'When I started out it was just me and a phone. If I didn't make a call then nothing would happen and that can be quite demoralising. So you have to make yourself pick up the phone and soon things start to happen. You come across things, meet people, have chance encounters and things happen – opportunities come your way.'

They certainly have for Michael Jackson, chairman of PartyGaming, founder of Elderstreet Investments and formerly chairman of software firm Sage, a business he led from having a £1m market capitalisation to one of £2bn.

Jackson was working in finance when Sage approached him, in the early 1980s and asked if he would help them find backers. They were looking for £350,000 and Jackson helped them get it. He also took 1% of Sage for £10,000.

One thing he's learned from working with Sage and his many other business interests is the importance of managing existing customers better. 'Too often it's all about chasing the next deal, the next big thing, but what Sage was very clever about was concentrating on how it could sell additional products and services to its existing clients. I think too often this is overlooked by businesses.'

As executive chairman of Elderstreet Investments, a company specialising in raising finance and investing in the smaller companies sector, Jackson has come across a wide range of businesses. He says the best ones have sound business models. 'That means they are not reliant on a small number of large clients; that they are selling stuff that people need rather than simply would like; and that they have a competitive advantage of some sort, either in terms of product or their customer service.'

Jackson is a director and investor in many other quoted and unquoted companies including, Planit Holdings, Netstore, Computer Software Group and Micromuse Inc. He says some companies fall down by over-complicating what they do. 'Doing a few things well is important,' he says. 'And so it's important to be disciplined.'

Jackson says that starting with nothing (albeit with a law degree from Cambridge) made him hungrier to succeed. The knowledge that without his efforts, no money would come in was a great motivator. He also understands that once a business is up and running that it is crucial to recruit top people. But it's not simple.

He explains:

'The best people aren't going to leave their jobs to come and work at a start-up just like that. So you have to pay the market rate or over the market rate to get them. And I did that – for a long time the people I employed were earning much more than me. You have to spend as much as you can, and give people options or shares in the business. Without the right quality of people you will never grow a successful business.'

Dawn Gibbins

'You need clear market focus'

Dawn Gibbins is founder of UK-based flooring specialist Flowcrete. The company makes floors for factories (Belgium), airports (UK, Malaysia), shopping centres (Shanghai, China; United Arab Emirates), schools (Scotland), offices (Sydney, Australia), stadiums (Coventry, UK), public spaces (Denmark; Latvia) and military establishments (UK). In fact, there's a good chance you've stood on one of Gibbins's floors.

She was the youngest ever industrialist to be awarded an MBE, now employs 350 people, runs eight factories, has 26 sales offices around the world and her clients include Panasonic, Pepsi and Intercontinental Hotels. Gibbins, it is fair to say, is one of life's enthusiasts.

'I've worked in this business for 25 years and there are three major areas that every company should concentrate on,' Gibbins says:

'First of all we specialise! In floors! I've been pulled in different directions over the years but we concentrate and are experts in floors. Think floors, think Flowcrete! Many of our competitors are more generalised but I think the specialisation gives us an edge because we have so much knowledge about floors.'

Secondly, she says:

'You need clear market focus. For the first 15 years we focussed on manufacturing plants for food or pharmaceutical companies, but with that market seeing a decline, in the UK at least, we started to move into public spaces, hospitals and schools. One thing that really helped me was going to business school. It helped us think about strategy and business planning and I'd highly recommend it.'

Third:

'You need to think about the languages you speak to people in. The people we speak to vary from construction firms to pharmaceutical companies to architects. Each has their own language and it is important to understand that. For example if we do a floor for a medical establishment they are most interested in hygiene issues. If we speak to construction firms they are focussed on profits. Architects have another language of things that are important to them, so with each group we make sure we talk in their language.'

Flowcrete runs seminars and training about floors for architects, as it realises that these people are those drawing up plans for new airports, factories or buildings – and they need the flooring expertise as much as Flowcrete wants the business.

But Flowcrete also innovates. 'We're working on Dublin airport. They wanted a more reflective flooring to chime in with all the green awareness and cutting back on energy use, so we came up with one using recycled mirrors. They loved it and we're now rolling it out worldwide.'

Employing good people has been a key to Flowcrete's success, Gibbins says, and she swears by psychometric testing.

*Gibbins sold Flowcrete in 2008 to US-based RPM International Inc

Deborah Meaden

'It's important to do what you say you are going to do'

In talking about the secrets to running a successful business, Deborah Meaden, the entrepreneurial investor on popular BBC TV show *Dragons' Den* says:

'I don't think there are any secrets to running a successful business. It really is a lot of common sense. Perhaps one reason I've done well is that I get stuff done. I do my homework, do my research, then get committed. I'm cool, calm and critical. But when I make a decision I always follow it through.'

Meaden is portrayed as something of a sourpuss but the reality couldn't be more different. Charming and funny in person, the reason for the TV persona is simple: 'If someone with only the vaguest grasp of business reality was asking you for £250,000 of your own money, you wouldn't be laughing either.'

One of Meaden's best early work experiences included running a prize bingo concession at British holiday park company Butlins. 'It was a real time and motion study,' she says. 'The more games we played the more money we made. It taught me not to waste words and keep the customers interested – because if they didn't like you or the service was poor, they could simply get up and walk off. It taught me all about customer service.'

She then took up a position in the family amusement arcade business before moving across into the holiday park side of the business, Weststar Holidays. Within two years she had been promoted to managing director and grew the company from one to five holiday parks.

Meaden recalls:

'In 2003, I was approached by some people who wanted to make me an offer for Weststar Holidays and early on we discussed and agreed on the price. At midnight the night before, they put in a lower offer thinking I would accept but I turned them down. That surprised them but that's me all over. I think many people, when they come to selling a business, are half thinking about retiring to sit on a beach and they will accept a last minute reduction in the offer. But not me – I wasn't heading to the beach. They misread me.'

She sold the business in 2005 in a deal worth £33m while retaining a 23% stake and an active role within the firm. She sold her remaining stake in the business when Weststar was sold to Parkdean Holidays for £83m.

For Meaden, business is simple. 'It's important to do what you say you are going to do,' she says. 'I also want people to push boundaries when they work for me. I'm happy for them to make mistakes if enough planning and research has gone into something.' She says it is important to reward people who do well for you, but also to tell people if they have done something wrong. 'I want people to know they have done something wrong,' she says.

'Ultimately, though, I have a lot of fun in business. Always have and always will. People don't think that about me when they see me on TV, but you couldn't work at a holiday park for all the years I did without having a sense of humour.'